Teams

Learning Made Simple

Lesley Partridge

ELSEVIER

AMSTERDAM • BOSTON • HEIDELBERG • LONDON • NEW YORK • OXFORD
PARIS • SAN DIEGO • SAN FRANCISCO • SINGAPORE • SYDNEY • TOKYO

Butterworth-Heinemann is an imprint of Elsevier

Butterworth-Heinemann is an imprint of Elsevier
Linacre House, Jordan Hill, Oxford OX2 8DP, UK
30 Corporate Drive, Suite 400, Burlington, MA 01803, USA

First edition 2007

Notice
No responsibility is assumed by the publisher for any injury and/or
damage to persons or property as a matter of products liability,
negligence or otherwise, or from any use or operation of any methods,
products, instructions or ideas contained in the material herein.

British Library Cataloguing in Publication Data
A catalogue record for this book is available from the British Library.

Library of Congress Cataloguing in Publication Data
A catalogue record for this book is available
from the Library of Congress.

ISBN: 978 0 7506 8451 4

For information on all Made Simple publications
visit our website at http://books.elsevier.com

Edited and typeset by P.K. McBride

Cartoons by John Leech

Icons designed by Sarah Ward © 1994

Printed and bound in MKT PRINT, Slovenia

Contents

Introduction v

1 Building effective teams   1

Why teams? 2

Benefits of teams 3

Diversity in teams 7

Diversity in team membership 13

Take the lead 15

2 Team development   19

Know the stages 20

Know team member roles 23

Use a team contract 27

3 Team performance   29

Introduction 30

Clarify purpose and goals 31

Encourage motivation 35

Focus on the task 37

Support the team 43

4 Communications   49

Communicate! 50

Listen 53

Use questions 57

Run effective team meetings 59

Manage the discussion 64

Use technology for communications 69

5   Team relationships   76

Build trust 77

Give and take feedback 82

Deal with conflict 86

Focus on the stakeholders 89

6   Collaboration   95

Solve problems in the team 96

Clarify the problem 102

Generate options 106

Assess the options 111

Make the decision 116

Implement and review 119

Index   121

Introduction

You can put the 'team' label on a group of people, but that doesn't make them a team.

This book gives you simple tips and ideas to get people working together as a team. It looks at key aspects of team building:

◆ Building effective teams – what makes a team and what the benefits are; different types of teams and being clear about the role of the leader.

◆ Team development – how teams develop; the team roles you need; agreeing a team contract.

◆ Team performance – how to establish shared goals; create the conditions for motivation; enable the team to carry out its work and support the team.

◆ Communications – the basics of communication together with all-important listening skills; how to run effective team meetings and use technological methods that make communication at a distance possible.

◆ Team relationships – how to build trust and support; giving and taking feedback constructively; how to resolve conflict and understand stakeholders.

◆ Collaboration – techniques and ideas for collaborating to solve problems and make decisions step by step.

It is designed primarily for team leaders and facilitators. But it is also useful for team members who are interested in making their team work well.

You can follow the structure of the book or dip into the chapters that most interest you. You will probably find that these lead you on to other chapters.

Lesley Partridge

2007

1 Building effective teams

Why teams? 2

Benefits of teams 3

Diversity in teams 7

Diversity in team membership 13

Take the lead 15

Why teams?

This first chapter looks at why teamwork is so popular. You'll find out that teams can bring significant benefits for individuals and for organisations.

What is a team?

This diagram represents a group of individuals at work:

Everyone is heading in a different direction, to achieve their individual objectives, and there is only a weak border to put them together as a group. In comparison, what does a successful team look like?

In this team everyone is contributing to move forward in a clear direction. Everyone works within the borders. Everyone works to achieve common, shared goals. They also work together, collaborating and co-operating, to enable them to make progress.

A team combines the energy, motivation, experiences and expertise of individuals for a shared purpose so that the team achieves more than the sum of the talents of its individual members.

Benefits and drawbacks

Benefits

Teamworking has a number of important benefits. In a team its members can:

- Have a sense of belonging
- Have a clear purpose and know what they have to achieve
- Feel supported by other team members
- Be respected and valued for their contribution
- Share problems and solve problems together.

I find it immensely satisfying being part of the team, both personally and professionally. We have developed good supportive working relationships, so we can talk about issues. And professionally, we have just had a series of very creative team meetings that has given us some exciting solutions.

An organisation can benefit from teams because:

- Everyone in a team is working towards the same goals
- It is clear how far a team is contributing to the wider goals of the organisation
- The mutual cooperation and support in teams enhance job satisfaction, which means people are likely to stay with the organisation
- The pooling of different levels and areas of expertise and experience can improve problem-solving and decision-making
- A team can largely plan and control its own work, rather than have control imposed on it.

Drawbacks

But teamworking does have drawbacks. Not everyone likes working in teams. People in creative professions, for example, are often fiercely individualistic and find it hard to fit happily within the team's borders.

A design school has a set of learning materials as the core body of knowledge for one of its courses. The course director has asked practising designers to act as tutors. She would like them to work as a team, supporting a common approach and ethos to the course. However, the designers all have their own design philosophy and take an individual approach to their subject. They tend to ignore the guidance given to tutors and have no second thoughts about undermining the authority of the course.

The other drawback is that effective teamworking doesn't happen automatically. People may say that they are part of a team, even when it actually doesn't have the two key characteristics of a team, which are people working together in a supportive way, to achieve shared goals.

> A team that isn't working as a team doesn't deliver the benefits.

Forging a team from a group of individuals takes time, effort and commitment. Attention has to be given to the teams and teamworking. At first this can detract from getting the job done, but when team members give consideration to the way they can and should work together, they can deliver the full potential of high performance.

Building effective teams

An effective team is one that has two key characteristics:

◆ People work together in a supportive way

◆ People work to achieve common goals.

With support of the company or organisation, managers, supervisors or team leaders can build effective teams. They need to:

◆ Understand team development and how to move a team forward

◆ Establish a clear purpose and shared goals

◆ Focus on performance

◆ Create high levels of commitment and motivation

◆ Ensure good, open communications

◆ Build trust in relationships

◆ Encourage team problem-solving and decision-making.

Activity

Assess the effectiveness of a team you belong to or lead. For each of these statements rate your team from 1–5 where 1 means 'we don't do this at all', and 5 means 'we do this well'. Place a tick in the appropriate column.

	1	2	3	4	5
Team development					
We take time to consider how we are working together	☐	☐	☐	☐	☐
We tend to play different team roles	☐	☐	☐	☐	☐
We have an active team contract	☐	☐	☐	☐	☐
Team performance					
We have clear, shared goals that contribute to the organisation	☐	☐	☐	☐	☐
There is a high level of motivation in the team	☐	☐	☐	☐	☐
Everyone works to clear, agreed objectives	☐	☐	☐	☐	☐
Team members monitor and review their progress	☐	☐	☐	☐	☐
Team members have plenty of opportunities to develop and use new skills	☐	☐	☐	☐	☐
We celebrate success	☐	☐	☐	☐	☐
Communications					
We communicate well as a team	☐	☐	☐	☐	☐
We take care to listen to each other	☐	☐	☐	☐	☐
We make good use of team meetings	☐	☐	☐	☐	☐
We use technological methods to communicate with team members who work at a distance	☐	☐	☐	☐	☐
Team relationships					
There is a high level of trust and support in the team	☐	☐	☐	☐	☐
People give and receive feedback constructively	☐	☐	☐	☐	☐
We deal with conflict openly	☐	☐	☐	☐	☐
We know our stakeholders' expectations and plan to meet them	☐	☐	☐	☐	☐
Collaboration					
We use a range of techniques to solve problems as a team	☐	☐	☐	☐	☐
We make decisions as a team	☐	☐	☐	☐	☐
We aim to learn from our experiences	☐	☐	☐	☐	☐

Now consider your results. Where have you placed most of your ticks? If most of your ticks are in columns 4 and 5 – towards the right-hand side of the page – the team is likely to be working effectively. Look for areas to improve and focus on these as you work through the book. If most of your ticks are in columns 1 and 2 – towards the left – there is plenty of scope to improve the team's effectiveness. If most of your ticks are in column 3, in the middle, the team may be working reasonably well, but it has the potential to do better.

This book looks at each of these areas in turn. You may want to focus on the areas where you feel there is most room for improvement in your team.

Go for early success to give your team the confidence to make further improvements.

Diversity in teams

Teams are diverse, both in type and in their membership.

The type of team may vary according to its:

◆ Purpose or function

◆ Composition

◆ Leadership structure.

Work teams

A work team is charged to carry out routine work. Its purpose will be ongoing, and probably accompanied by periodic targets for performance. The people in the team may perform different functions, or they may have similar functions but different levels of experience and expertise. Examples of work teams could include:

◆ Call centre teams

◆ Customer service teams

◆ Engineering maintenance teams

◆ Sales support teams.

Some work teams could more properly be called work groups. In a work group the members operate independently. They are working to achieve individual objectives and although these may contribute to a set of overall goals for the group, the members have little reason for formal communication with each other.

A work group's structure may look like this:

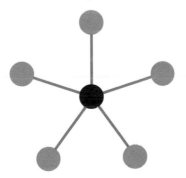

Here the leader in the centre typically has authority over the other members because of his or her position; he or she is the boss. The leader communicates directly with individuals and the group as a whole. But there is no formal contact between members. Here is an example:

The sales staff in the East Anglian regional sales team of a drinks company mostly sell to the area's pubs and restaurants. They all have individual sales targets and operate independently developing and maintaining good customer relationships under the leadership of a regional sales manager. The sales staff all contribute to the region's overall targets.

The manager holds regular team meetings with staff briefing them on new products and new customer relationships, and working with individuals on development issues. There is a lot of informal and friendly communication between the sales staff.

In a work team, on the other hand, team members are dependent on each other. They must work together to achieve their individual objectives and the team's goals.

The next example shows how a work group changed its working practices to operate more as a team:

After restructuring at a call centre, call operators now work in teams to encourage better motivation and more job satisfaction. Each team has its own work area, set apart from other teams, and a team leader. Team members handle calls individually, but their bonuses and pay incentives are closely linked to the overall performance of the team. This has changed the way operators work.

Team members meet regularly to review progress towards team targets, solve problems and agree action, such as coverage during periods of heavy call traffic. Experienced operators help to develop less experienced team members, and everyone in the team provides mutual support and encouragement, for example, giving a team member time to talk about a difficult call.

In work teams where team members have different but complementary skills, the team members must collaborate, working cooperatively and contributing their skills and expertise to get the work done.

A team structure typically looks like this:

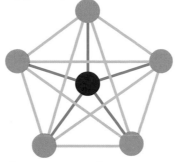

Again, the leader has a central position and is likely have positional authority over the members. The leader communicates with everyone in the team, but members also communicate directly with each other.

The members of a work team may be located together, sharing offices or a work site. However, flexible working is common and individuals may work flexible hours or part-time, they may job share, they may work from home as teleworkers. Some members may be temporary or subcontracted to the team. In international and global organisations work teams may be made up from people working in different countries. A team may include members from different nationalities.

A key leadership role is to make sure that all team members feel part of the team, no matter what their working arrangements are. Communication will be of particular importance.

Project teams

A project team is established for a single purpose, and once that is achieved it can be disbanded. Here are some examples:

◆ To investigate and report on outsourcing part of the company's production to Poland.

◆ To install and set up new equipment and machinery.

◆ To join with members of the local community to plan and run a fundraising event for a local children's hospice.

◆ To set up a new intranet for the company.

◆ To recommend how a company can reach a new market.

◆ To take part in a joint venture with partnership organisations to design and launch a new service.

A project team brings together a variety of technical or subject expertise in order to achieve its goals. So it may well be composed of people from a range of:

◆ **Professional backgrounds and cultures** – For example, a team may include a marketing professional, an engineer, and an accountant.

◆ **Levels of authority** – Team members may hold different positions of power and seniority in an organisation or have different levels of expertise and experience, e.g. a team may include a marketing professional and a marketing assistant.

◆ **Affiliations** – Team members may be independent consultants or may come from different organisations.

◆ **Locations** – A project team may operate locally, but equally members may be scattered over a wide geographic area.

Given the potentially diverse composition of project teams, the leader may not be the most senior member and may have no positional authority over the others. There are two main team structures and leadership roles:

◆ The team leader has responsibility for achieving the project's goals, and the project team is set up to help the team leader to do this. The team leader is the boss of the project, but is not the team members' boss. He or she doesn't have responsibility for developing individuals, and the focus is likely to be on getting the team working well in order to achieve the task in hand. The structure may well look like this:

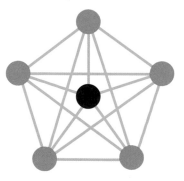

◆ The team structure may be democratic – a set of equals, with the leader appointed by consent, because of that person's ability to build a team. The leadership role is to facilitate the team's ability to work effectively and achieve its goals.

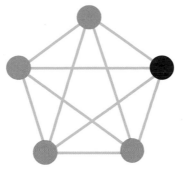

The facilitator takes on leadership functions, such as coordinating and supporting, but crucially does not make decisions or influence decision-making. The facilitator aims to help the team to make its own decisions.

Quality improvement teams

A quality improvement team has a long-term life, like the work team, and may have a similar composition, made up from people who are also members of relevant work teams. However, its function is to identify areas for improvement and use team problem-solving and decision-making to plan, carry out and review improvements. Improvement teams may be structured democratically as suggested in the project team, or it may have a leader who has positional authority over team members.

Self-managed teams

In a self-managed team there is no leader. Some management experts have argued that as the team develops its teamworking skills and ability to manage and control its own workload, a leader becomes less important or even unnecessary, making the self-managed team the ultimate development for teams.

However, teams continue to need someone to take on leadership functions to facilitate and coordinate the team's work. So in self-managed teams the team members either share the leadership functions or take turns in the leadership role. This can put a burden on team members to develop leadership skills, which may explain why self-managed teams are not common. They are more likely to occur in project teams than in work teams.

Virtual teams

A virtual team exists when its members are in different geographical areas, perhaps spread globally across time zones. They may meet only rarely or perhaps never meet face-to-face at all. The dispersed nature of the team brings particular challenges in terms of effective communications and forging a team. A virtual team is also likely to be a project team.

Activity

Think of one or two teams to which you belong, either as a member or as a leader. For each, identify what type it is. Briefly describe its characteristics in terms of its:

◆ Purpose or function – consider the expected life of the team.

◆ Composition – think about where team members work, their levels of expertise or influence.

◆ Leadership structure – does the leader have positional authority or is the leader's role to coordinate and facilitate?

Does your description highlight the need to pay attention to any of these aspects of teamworking:

◆ The way the team agrees to work together?

◆ Methods and processes for communicating?

◆ Effectiveness of team meetings?

◆ Leadership role and functions?

◆ Development of the team?

◆ Techniques for team problem-solving and decision-making?

You may want to focus on these aspects as you work through this book.

Diversity in team membership

Teams are often characterised by diversity in their members. Diversity means difference. We have already seen potential sources of difference among team members:

◆ Professional background and culture – the culture of a nurse will be different from that of a journalist and different again from that of an engineer.

◆ Level of authority or formal influence.

◆ Working arrangements – hours, work location.

◆ Affiliation beyond the team – to an organisation, a professional body, trade union or other staff representative.

In addition team members will have personal differences:

◆ Gender

◆ Life style, such as family life, interests, financial position, etc.

◆ Age

◆ Sexual orientation

◆ Special needs

◆ Personality

◆ Values and beliefs

◆ Cultural, national or ethnic background.

Value in diversity

There was once a tendency in organisations to recruit people who shared a similar education, history and background. The idea was that they would fit in easily and quickly and feel comfortable in the organisation's culture. However, apart from the likelihood of illegally discriminating against people who are simply different, such an approach was short-sighted:

◆ In a society that includes many different cultures, it gave organisations a shrinking pool of people from which to recruit.

- Like-minded people tend to have similar views – which meant decisions were made from a narrow perspective that did not always appreciate their customers' changing requirements or interests.

In contrast, a diverse team reflects the values and opinions of their equally diverse customers. This is valuable for a number of reasons:

- Team members bring in widely different perspectives, which enables the team to understand and respond to customers.

- The contribution of different perspectives leads to creative problem-solving and decision-making.

- A diverse team is likely to be flexible and open to the need to learn and change.

However, the individuality and difference among teams can be a source of tension when team members have to be team players – cooperating and contributing to common goals.

The team has to accommodate and value individual differences while fostering a commitment to the team goals and team approach. The team leader can play a key role in this.

Take the lead

Building an effective team takes leadership.

From manager to leader

It is interesting that the language surrounding teams rarely includes 'managers'. Traditional management functions include:

- Planning
- Organising
- Controlling
- Directing
- Coordinating
- Monitoring
- Reviewing.

The emphasis is on the manager's role to control and direct the efforts of staff to achieve the task.

This has changed partly to reflect changing expectations and requirements in the workplace and in society as a whole:

- It is generally accepted that people are more motivated to perform well if they have some responsibility and control for their own work, in other words they take ownership of their job. This means that individuals carry out some of the management functions themselves.

- Acceptance of authority has changed in our society over the last 50 years or so. People are generally less willing to take direction from a manager. They are more likely to question what they are doing and to need to know why they should do something.

- Change, whether technological or in customer requirements or in social attitudes, mean that organisations need to be able to respond quickly if they are to remain competitive and retain their customers.

◆ New, less hierarchical organisations mean that those with positional authority in an organisation do not always have the specialist expertise of their staff.

These changes have led to a recognition of the importance of teams and the leadership role. With their diverse composition, teams are flexible and able to take on many of the management functions to control and plan their own work. But in order to develop these skills and become effective, teams need a leader.

Teams and leadership

There are three elements in a team:

◆ **The task** – what the team is expected to achieve

◆ **The team** – how team members cooperate and collaborate as a team to achieve the task

◆ **The individual** – how individuals contribute both to the team and the task.

The leader's role is concerned with enabling the team to achieve the results required. Some leaders will focus on all three elements: task, team and individual. Others will focus on only one or two of these elements. The focus of the leader's role will depend on the type of team he or she is leading:

◆ The team leader who is the team members' boss – typically in a work team – will focus on all three elements: task, team and individual.

◆ The leader who is the boss of the job, but not the team members' superior – typically in a project team – will focus on the task and the team.

◆ The facilitator whose purpose is to ensure its smooth running and help it to make its own decisions will focus on the team.

◆ The team member who takes on leadership functions to help the team develop and perform – typically in a self-managed team – will focus on the team.

The next activity asks you to identify the functions that you perform in your role as a leader.

Think about a team in which you have or are about to take a leadership role – identify the type of team that it is and your role as a leader.

The chart below lists some of the key leadership functions across the three elements of task, team and individual. For each function tick the appropriate column to show whether or not you perform or will need to perform it.

Leadership functions	Do you or will you do this?		
	Yes	No	Don't know
Create clear shared goals and help the team keep a focus on these	☐	☐	☐
Coordinate work	☐	☐	☐
Take on management functions, where appropriate, e.g. initiating action, taking decisions, reviewing progress	☐	☐	☐
Promote problem-solving and decision-making	☐	☐	☐
Develop an atmosphere of trust and mutual support in the team	☐	☐	☐
Encourage open two-way communications	☐	☐	☐
Help the team develop and perform	☐	☐	☐
Help individuals develop and perform	☐	☐	☐
Create conditions that allow people to be committed to their work	☐	☐	☐
Encourage participation and involvement	☐	☐	☐
Support people in achieving their goals	☐	☐	☐

If you don't know, then talk to your manager or the person who is appointing you to the role.

Now think about your level of confidence and competence in performing those functions you perform.

Whatever functions you perform as a team leader, your team will look to you to set the atmosphere of the team. You can set a positive atmosphere by showing commitment to developing and improving your skills as a team leader. This book will help you to do this as you work to build your team.

Summary

◆ A team combines the energy, motivation, experiences and expertise of individuals for a shared purpose so that the team achieves more than the sum of the talents of its individual members.

◆ Teams benefit team members – they create an atmosphere of mutual support and respect.

◆ Organisations also benefit from teams because of the mutual support and cooperation in achieving shared goals.

◆ A team that isn't working effectively as a team doesn't deliver the benefits.

◆ Team leaders can build effective teams by:

  ❖ Understanding team development, and how to move a team forward

  ❖ Establishing a clear purpose and shared goals

  ❖ Focusing on performance

  ❖ Creating high levels of commitment and motivation

  ❖ Ensuring good, open communications

  ❖ Building trust in team relationships

  ❖ Encouraging team problem-solving and decision-making.

◆ Teams vary in their purpose, composition and leadership structure.

◆ Types of teams include work teams, project teams, quality improvement teams, self-managed teams, virtual teams.

◆ One of the key benefits of teams is the diversity in their composition. Different perspectives are valuable because they can enhance decision-making.

◆ The leader's role is concerned with enabling the team to achieve the results required, but the functions leaders carry out will depend on the type of team they lead.

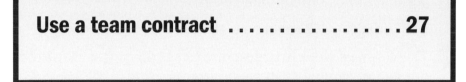

2 Team development

Know the stages **20**

Know team member roles **23**

Use a team contract **27**

Through creating it had been a little time consuming, all the ants agreed that the contract was a good idea

Know the stages

There are three central components to teamwork:

◆ The task – what the team is charged to achieve

◆ The individuals – the members of the team

◆ The team itself – the way it operates.

To benefit fully from teamwork, the team must be operating effectively. This doesn't happen automatically and teams tend to go through recognisable stages before they reach maturity and optimum performance. There are different ways of describing the stages that teams go through to get there, but one of the most useful, if partly because it is so memorable is:

Forming   Storming   Norming   Performing

These stages were first described in 1965 by B.W. Tuckman in 'Developmental sequences in small groups' in *Psychological Bulletin* 63.

Forming

When a team is first put together, its members are likely to want to find out about the purpose of the team and the role they are expected to play. Questions team members are exploring at this stage are:

◆ What's my role?

◆ How do I fit in?

◆ What are we expected to achieve?

◆ What resources do we have?

◆ Can we do it?

◆ How should we communicate and work together?

Storming

Team members move from questioning to seeking agreement on purpose and goals and how to achieve them. Members may challenge the team's purpose, composition and its leadership. As they are still working out how to work together, this stage is often characterised by disagreement and conflict. This can impede the further development of the team unless conflict is resolved to team members' satisfaction, meeting their individual interests and concerns.

Norming

Team members recognise the need to agree ground rules in order to operate as a team. The team's culture and customs, the way its members will operate and collaborate become established practice. Team members are still likely to disagree at this stage, but they tend to be more positive and able to work together.

Performing

The team is able to perform effectively, delivering the benefits team-work can bring. Team members have the confidence and commitment needed to work cooperatively towards their shared team goals. The emphasis is on achieving the team's goals.

Activity

At what stage is your team operating? Use these questions to help you to decide.

◆ What are the team's current activities and its concerns?

◆ How much conflict is there?

◆ Do disagreements tend to be about how best to achieve the team's goals, as they may be in the performing stage – or are they about the way team members are collaborating and cooperating?

◆ Has a new task or a new member changed the way the team operates?

These stages provide a general guide to the way teams tend to develop, not a rigid prescription. A team can move through the stages quite rapidly, or it can get stuck at a particular stage. You may find that there is some fluidity between the stages, and that a team seems to make progress to another stage and then seems to revert, particularly when it is faced with a new task that is outside its usual experience, or if the composition of the team changes.

Your aim as a team leader will be to help the team to progress through the stages so that it is able to perform well and keep performing well.

Moving through the stages

The team's concerns and priorities are different at each stage. When a team is formed, team members are concerned about the individual as part of a team – how they will fit into the team, for example. Concern with how the team will work becomes more important as the team moves into the storming and norming stages. During the norming stage the team can start to give real attention to the task. But it is not until the performing stage that the team is able to prioritise the task and work effectively. The diagram below shows how the emphasis changes as the team develops.

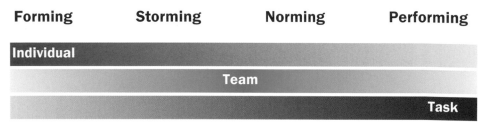

You can help the team to move through the stages by dealing with the team's primary concerns as they emerge.

This doesn't mean that you have to ignore the purpose – task – of the team at the early stages. In fact you can use the task as the focal point around which individuals sort out their role in the team and work out how they can operate effectively as a team. But in the early stages of team development, progress on achieving the task tends to be slow and subordinated to other concerns.

Know team member roles

Individuals often join a team to fulfil a functional role that is needed to achieve the team's goals or its task. The functional role tends to be linked to a person's expertise and the job he or she does, salesperson, website designer, electronics engineer and so on. These roles are usually visible or obvious, perhaps given in job descriptions or in the way people describe themselves.

When people work together in teams they tend naturally to adopt other roles depending on their personality, priorities and interests with regard to the task and their interaction with people. For example, someone may be a peacemaker; another may be an ideas person, thinking creatively; someone else may tend to question and challenge; another may be concerned with getting the job finished.

Such roles are important to the way the team operates and its overall effectiveness. They tend to centre around the following:

◆ Keeping the team going

  ❖ Being supportive

  ❖ Encouraging contributions from everyone and seeking ideas and opinions

  ❖ Seeking friendly agreement or compromise

  ❖ Being positive

  ❖ Reviewing how the team is operating

◆ Keeping a focus on the team's goals and objectives

  ❖ Taking the initiative – making suggestions and offering direction

  ❖ Seeking and providing information

  ❖ Clarifying objectives and ideas

  ❖ Challenging ideas

  ❖ Summarising

  ❖ Checking progress

❖   Meeting deadlines

❖   Working with others outside the team.

> Team roles are concerned with maintaining the team and achieving the task.

Complementary roles

There has been much research and discussion on the roles people play in teams, and researchers have argued that in successful teams there is a balanced mix of people each taking different but complementary roles that help the team perform effectively.

There are various descriptions of the key team roles, but Meredith Belbin's team roles is one of the most well-known:

Belbin's team roles

Shaper: directs and stimulates action and can overcome problems or obstacles; energetic and driven to succeed.

Plant: is an innovative, creative thinker; individualistic and unconventional.

Monitor-evaluator: is an analytical, critical thinker; cautious and detached.

Resource investigator: is good at exploring, investigating and communicating and at responding to challenges; curious and enthusiastic.

Coordinator: keeps a focus on objectives and makes the most of the skills and resources available in and to the team; self-confident and in control.

Implementer: is reliable, efficient and organised and does the work that needs to be done; practical and disciplined.

Teamworker: is concerned with personal relationships; provides support and encouragement and acts as a harmonising influence; sociable and diplomatic.

Completer-finisher: is concerned with attention to detail, high standards, following through and meeting deadlines; conscientious and meticulous.

Specialist: provides technical and specialist knowledge and skills to the team; expert in their field.

Belbin's research suggests that people have a tendency or preference to adopt one or two specific roles when part of a team, and that it is possible to identify people's natural behavioural tendencies through simple questionnaires or psychometric tests.

These tests can help to:

◆ Increase people's self-awareness

◆ Improve members' understanding of everyone's behaviour

◆ Provide information when recruiting to teams and building teams.

I was dubious about team roles until I managed a team that was full of creative thinkers and critical thinkers – it was very difficult to make any progress at all. Now I actively seek to create a balance of team roles in the composition of my team. When we are missing a key role I look for a team member who can take it on without bending them out of shape too much.

To find out more about Belbin's team roles and taking psychometric tests to identify your natural team roles, visit Belbin Associates website.

Activity

Consider the way a team you belong to or lead is operating.

◆ What roles are your team members playing in keeping the team going and in making progress toward the team's objectives?

◆ You may be able to identify the roles people tend to adopt by:

❖ Observing what they say and do, and looking for patterns

❖ Talking to any colleagues who know your team members

❖ Considering their background and experience, as shown in job applications, appraisals and performance reviews, for instance

❖ Asking what they prefer to do

❖ Using a psychometric test, such as Belbin's, with everyone in the team to help identify preferred roles.

◆ What roles, if any, are missing from your team?

◆ What effect do you think this is having on your team?

There are several ways of filling any missing roles in your team:

◆ Recruiting new members

◆ Identifying team members who may be able to take on these roles and asking them to fill them

◆ Discussing team roles with the team and ways in which team members can contribute to

    ❖ Keeping the team going

    ❖ Keeping a focus on the team's goals and objectives.

Team roles could be part of your team contract.

Use a team contract

A useful way of highlighting the importance of the way the team operates is to explore and agree ground rules with team members and draw these up in a team contract.

The team contract or constitution is a document that sets out how team members want to work together. It can establish its values, policies, procedures and rules. It is intended to be an active document: team members can refer to it at appropriate times to check how far they are following the rules and their expectations. They can also change and update the contract if it doesn't seem to be serving a useful purpose for the team.

Team members can decide what to put into the contract, whatever will help them to be productive. The following are some ideas to consider:

Ideas for drawing up a team contract

◆ Ask team members what they expect from the experience of being part of a team.

◆ Identify the core values of the team. This may be related to the team's purpose and its overall role in the organisation.

◆ Think about meeting procedures – when the team will meet, preparation, who attends, how people participate, outcomes of the meeting. For example, is an agenda to be agreed and issued before each meeting? Who will record the meeting and how?

◆ Consider procedures and codes of conduct to promote effective communication among team members.

◆ Consider how the team will deal with disagreements and conflict.

◆ Think about ways of building team spirit and creating a pleasant team atmosphere – for example you may order in pizza for lunch when there is a team meeting or organise informal social events.

The team contract is an opportunity to agree how to behave, communicate, meet and work together. Here is how one team leader led his team to develop a team contract.

Case study

I'm the new team leader of a customer service team. At an early team meeting, I ran a session to develop a team contract. We looked at 'what we are here to do', and how we contribute to the organisation. Then we did a brainstorm to choose a suitable motto for the team. This lightened the tone, but it proved to be a useful way of getting a picture of the team's values. The team came up with:

'To our customers, we are the company'.

From this we started to identify the team rules or guidelines. We decided to keep them short and simple:

'We are always considerate to each other

We keep informed and up to date

We all work to achieve our targets

We all contribute equally

We are ready to learn and develop.'

Summary

◆ Teams tend to go through stages of development to reach maturity. These can be described as:

Forming   Storming   Norming   Performing.

You can help the team move through the stages.

◆ Everyone in a team will have a functional or technical role, but they will also adopt team roles in the way they work with other team members.

◆ Effective team roles tend to centre around:

❖ Keeping the team going

❖ Keeping a focus on the team's goals and objectives.

◆ It is important to consider whether you have an appropriate mix of roles in your team and find ways of creating the balance you need.

◆ The team contract encourages members to think about the processes involved in teamworking and to specify how they want to work as a team.

3 Team performance

Introduction 30

Clarify purpose and goals 31

Encourage motivation 35

Focus on the task 37

Support the team 43

Despite friends in the city receiving six figure bonuses, Pete
was more than happy with the offer of a boiled sweet

Introduction

In order to help your team to perform well you need to do the following:

◆ Ensure understanding and agreement of the team's purpose and goals.

◆ Encourage people to be motivated to put in the effort and commitment needed in their work.

◆ Enable team members to take responsibility for their work by involving them in:

  ❖ Setting and agreeing objectives

  ❖ Planning their work

  ❖ Implementing

  ❖ Monitoring their progress and taking corrective action when necessary.

  ❖ Reviewing.

◆ Support the team by:

  ❖ Being a team advocate

  ❖ Keeping team members informed of the bigger picture

  ❖ Encouraging development

  ❖ Integrating new team members

  ❖ Celebrating success.

In this chapter you look at each of these aspects of supporting team performance in turn.

Clarify purpose and goals

◆   Why does your team exist?

◆   What does it contribute to the organisation?

◆   What does it need to achieve?

These are important questions for a team to answer: they give direction, purpose and value to its work. Team members should be clear about its purpose and goals, and how by achieving them they are adding value to the organisation and benefiting personally as well.

Team purpose

One way of identifying why your team exists is to consider what it has to do. You can look at your team as a simple system:

◆   Suppliers are the organisations, teams and individuals that provide the inputs that the team requires.

◆   Inputs are all the resources the team needs to do its work – skills, expertise, effort, information, materials, equipment, finance.

◆   Team processes are the activities and operations that the team carries out to combine and transform its inputs in order to produce outputs.

◆   Outputs are everything the team produces – services, products, waste.

◆   Customers are the people, teams and organisations who use or require the team's outputs.

Consider your team as a simple system. Identify its:

◆ Suppliers

◆ Inputs

◆ Processes

◆ Outputs

◆ Customers.

By breaking down your team's work in this way, you should build a clear picture of why the team exists. Next, consider how it adds value to the organisation.

The organisational context

Organisations require everyone in the organisation to be working in the same direction towards the same goals.

You can see what an organisation is seeking to achieve in its mission, vision and value statements, if these exist. The mission summarises the organisation's purpose - why it exists; the vision identifies what it intends to be in the future - its ambitions and aspirations; and its values state the principles and beliefs that guide its activities. Even when an organisation does not clearly state these, they are usually evident in its publicity.

The organisation's strategy is what the organisation plans to do to achieve its mission and vision. Together the mission, vision, values and strategy are its overall goals.

These organisational goals become the basis for setting goals and plans in every part and level of the organisation. Business units, departments and teams all work out what the organisation's goals mean to them and what they must do to contribute effectively to achieving these goals. This approach is known as a hierarchy of objectives; it links the whole organisation together to achieve the same overall goals.

Hierarchy of objectives

Vision, Mission, Strategy

Department goals, objectives and plans

Team goals, objectives and plans

Activity

Think about whether your team members are all working (directly or indirectly) for the same organisation that is sponsoring and paying for the team, or whether it is a result of several organisations working together to achieve the same ends.

Look at what the organisation or organisations want to achieve. Consider their vision, mission and strategy. Then look at how the team is able and expected to contribute to these goals and aims.

Clear, shared goals

A statement of the team's goals shows what it has to achieve and how it is actively contributing to the overall goals of the organisation.

> In an effective team all team members are committed to achieving these goals.

This implies that team members:

◆ Are involved in establishing the team's goals

◆ Understand why they are needed

◆ Understand what they mean for the team and for team members personally

◆ Agree that they will serve their purpose, are important and worthwhile

◆ Feel that they will benefit personally by contributing to these goals.

Of course, your organisation may have set up the team to achieve a purpose and specific goals. In such a case you may feel that the team has no scope to develop shared goals – team members simply have to accept the ones it is given. However, this is not so.

Consider imposed team goals as providing the basis for developing team goals. You can explore, interpret and build on them with your team. Work with the team to establish shared goals that have meaning for all team members and that they are able to support and work wholeheartedly to achieve.

To establish shared goals

◆ Identify the team's purpose – its mission.

◆ Clarify where the team wants to go and what it wants to achieve – its vision.

◆ Identify how the team fits into the organisation and contributes to its goals.

◆ Encourage team members to consider how the team can help them meet their own goals. These may be to do with gaining new experience and skills, working with interesting people, contributing to something worthwhile, etc.

◆ Explore the values that are important to team members and that should guide the team's activities and behaviour. Values can include beliefs, principles, standards of behaviour, codes of conduct.

◆ Take stock of where the team is now – its current situation. For example, what is its current stage of development? What activities is it currently carrying out?

◆ Identify what the team has to do to go from where it is now to where it wants to go.

◆ Put the team goals in writing and review them – make sure that everyone shares them and agrees to them.

◆ Check that team goals meet the requirements of your organisation, customers and suppliers.

You can use the techniques of collaboration to establish team goals, and to promote team development (see Chapter 6). A statement of agreed team goals can also form part of a team contract.

Encourage motivation

Picture two teams in the same organisation:

◆ In the first, team members put in the hours, but little else. They aren't interested in their work and just do the bare minimum to get by. They drag their feet and watch the clock.

◆ In the second, team members are enthusiastic about what they are doing. They want to put energy and effort into their work and they think it is worth striving to achieve the team's goals.

It's not hard to see which team you'd like to have on your side. The second team is motivated – committed and involved in its work. It is clearly performing better than the poor first team. As a team leader you can't make people motivated – motivation is a personal inner drive – but you can do a lot to create the conditions that allow motivation to flourish.

What motivates people to work?

'Money' is the immediate reply from most people. We need money and the lack of it can be a strong motivator. But when we have money, its power to motivate is surprisingly low – the members in the teams described above are all paid for their work, but some are motivated and others aren't. So the things that drive us to achieve go beyond money.

Given the connection between motivation and high performance, it's not surprising that management theorists and researchers, working mainly in the 1950s to the 1970s, were interested in answering this question. Their findings suggest that people can be motivated by:

◆ A sense of achievement and personal satisfaction

◆ Doing something worthwhile

◆ Recognition of their contribution

◆ Control over their work

◆ An ability to make progress

◆ A sense of belonging

◆ A feeling that they are valued and respected.

Go through these factors in turn and tick the ones that motivate you.

How motivated are you at the moment? What are the reasons for this? If you have a low level of motivation, what factors do you feel are missing?

Now think about your team members and suggest which of these factors motivates them. Consider the effects of your level of motivation on the team.

Everyone is different and people are motivated by different things. But you probably agree that these factors can have a significant impact on people's motivation.

It is worth considering the effect of your own level of motivation on your team. As a team leader your team are likely to see you as a role model. If you show commitment and energy in your work, you are in a better position to enthuse others.

How to create a motivating environment

The chart below shows what you can do to help team members experience these motivating factors in their work.

Motivating factors	What you can do
A sense of achievement and personal satisfaction	Agree clear objectives so that team members can see what they have achieved
Doing something worthwhile	Agree meaningful objectives that contribute to the organisation's goals and values
Recognition of their contribution	Thank and praise team members; give positive feedback
Control over their work	Give team members responsibility for their work
An ability to make progress	Enable team members to develop and broaden their experiences; give constructive feedback
A sense of belonging	Encourage teamwork and collaboration and promote good working relationships
A feeling that they are valued and respected	Show that you respect and value team members in your relationships with them

Focus on the task

Let's look now at how to encourage motivation by involving people in their work, giving them responsibility to achieve the team's goals and supporting the team. Later we will look at ways of encouraging people to feel that they belong to the team and are valued and respected.

This diagram summarises the cycle to plan and control work to achieve agreed objectives.

The work cycle

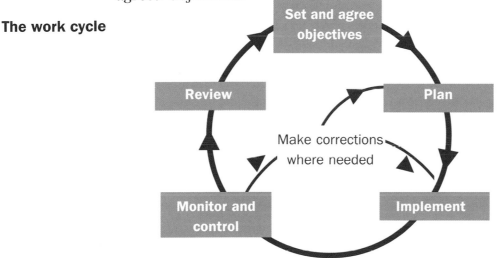

In the old managerial model of work, managers would be responsible for planning and controlling work. They would allocate work to the people who could do it, and monitor their performance.

Leaders may still be accountable for the work of the team but their role is likely to be to encourage team members to participate in planning and controlling and to take some responsibility for their own work.

This has significant benefits:

◆ It shows respect for the skills and judgement of the people who do the work.

◆ People feel able to control what they need to achieve and how they will do it, so they are more likely to be involved and engaged in their work. They are the people who are doing the work so are in the best position to realise straight away when there are problems or obstacles that can impede progress, and take action to correct the situation.

◆ Leaders don't need to be able to do the work of everyone in the team; they can draw on their expertise and experience, while providing appropriate support.

To enable team members to take some control for their work, team leaders need to judge how much instruction, guidance and support to give to team members. In other words, they must choose an appropriate leadership style.

Leadership style

The situational leadership model was developed by K. Blanchard and P. Hersey in 1973 (*Management of Organizational Behavior*, Prentice-Hall, 1977). It suggests four main styles: you should choose your style to match the needs of the task and the needs of your team members – their competence and willingness. A simple way of looking at this is that the higher these levels, the more the team leader is able to release control and direction for the task.

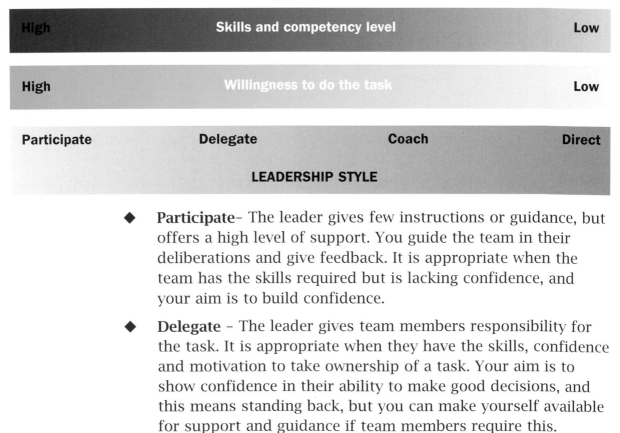

High	Skills and competency level	Low

High	Willingness to do the task	Low

Participate	Delegate	Coach	Direct

LEADERSHIP STYLE

◆ **Participate**– The leader gives few instructions or guidance, but offers a high level of support. You guide the team in their deliberations and give feedback. It is appropriate when the team has the skills required but is lacking confidence, and your aim is to build confidence.

◆ **Delegate** – The leader gives team members responsibility for the task. It is appropriate when they have the skills, confidence and motivation to take ownership of a task. Your aim is to show confidence in their ability to make good decisions, and this means standing back, but you can make yourself available for support and guidance if team members require this.

- **Coach** – The leader guides the team members through the process of planning and controlling work, providing instruction and support. You can encourage their contribution by seeking their ideas and opinions. It is appropriate when the team is developing the skills required.

- **Direct** – The leader gives clear instructions on what and how to do a task and monitors progress closely. It is appropriate when team members do not have the skills required and may be anxious or unwilling to take on the job. This may be the style to use if decisions need to be made rapidly: consultation takes time.

Setting and agreeing objectives

Objectives set out what needs to be achieved. Clear objectives:

- Give team members a strong direction

- Allow team members to monitor progress towards achieving their objectives

- Make visible the link between their efforts and what they achieve.

Objectives can be agreed at team level, then expanded to individual level. They can be motivational, especially if they are framed so they are SMART and are agreed with the people who have to achieve them.

SMART objectives

SMART objectives are called after the first letter of each of the criteria:

- **S**pecific – stating precisely what needs to be achieved

- **M**easurable – containing measures or standards so that everyone can keep track of progress and see when they have succeeded

- **A**chievable – they are feasible and realistic given the resources available

- **R**elevant – they contribute to the overall team goals

- **T**ime-bound – with deadlines against which progress can be measured and a completion date.

A call centre team has a goal to improve customer satisfaction with its service. To this end one of its objectives is to:

◆ Reduce call-waiting time by 10 per cent by the end of May.

How SMART is this objective?

The objective is specific and measurable – the team knows what is required and the measure for success (10 per cent reduction). There is a deadline and it is clearly relevant to the overall goal. It is not clear how achievable it is; that depends on the skills and resources available and also on the commitment of the team members. This highlights the needs for team members to agree to their objectives. By agreeing to and accepting their objectives they are more likely to be willing and committed to achieving them.

> To gain commitment encourage team members to take ownership of their objectives. Agree SMART objectives with those who are going to carry them out.

The way you agree objectives with your team and its members can encourage motivation. Choose an appropriate leadership style to match people's level of skill and willingness to be involved. For example, you may take a coaching approach with those who are keen to be involved, but who don't have the skills or experience in setting objectives. This way you can encourage them to take some responsibility. Discuss the objectives – guiding the team members to think through what needs to be achieved, ask them to make a draft of SMART objectives and then jointly review and finally agree the objectives.

Activity

Choose and use an appropriate leadership style to agree SMART objectives with your team members according to their skills and willingness to be involved. Review what happens:

◆ How far are team members committed to achieving their objectives?

◆ Are the objectives SMART?

◆ What could you do differently next time?

When you have agreed objectives with team members they can develop work plans.

Planning, monitoring and controlling

The role of the team leader will depend on the level of direction, support and guidance people require to plan, monitor and control their work. Even when using the delegating style – providing the lowest levels of direction and support – you will have a briefing discussion. This may cover the following:

◆ **Objectives**. Check that they are SMART.

◆ **Ways of doing the task**. Discuss how the team member plans to work to achieve the objectives and provide guidance and advice as appropriate.

◆ **The scope and constraints of the task**. Show how the task fits into the bigger picture of the department and organisation.

◆ **Resource requirements**, availability and how to access resources. You may be able to give team members access to particular resources or to other expertise in the organisation.

◆ **Ways of monitoring and reviewing work**, such as what aspects of the work to monitor and when, and providing information on progress.

◆ **Support and advice** available from you and others.

> Plans show how to do the work, and provide a means for monitoring resource use.

Reviewing

Reviewing is a key activity. Reflecting on what happened and why, and considering alternative approaches help people to learn.

Activity

When do you take part in or lead reviews?

Reviews can be formal or informal. Formal reviews include appraisals, end-of-project evaluation or reports. An informal review can take place at any time.

Regular progress reviews are important for monitoring progress and taking decisions on modifying plans, increasing resources or rewriting objectives.

But it is important to take the opportunity for a final review when the task has been completed. The final review can evaluate the task and provide valuable lessons for the future.

Here is a set of questions that you could use or adapt for a review session:

Review questions

- What were our objectives?

- How far did we achieve them?

- What are the consequences of this level of success for us and for others, e.g. our customers?

- How did we plan to achieve our objectives?

- What went well?

- What difficulties or obstacles did we face?

- Why did they occur?

- What action did we take in response?

- What factors influenced our actions?

- What factors should we have taken into account?

- How does everyone feel about what happened? How did people feel at the time?

- What are the key lessons that we can learn from what happened?

- What will we do the same or differently next time?

Support the team

Effective teams give each other mutual support. This support can be practical, providing resources and assistance to do a job; showing interest in each other's work, discussing issues and concerns and helping someone to find the best way of tackling an aspect of their work, for instance. Support can also be emotional – showing a concern and interest in fellow team members.

Here is an example:

Help line team member:

Unhappy customers can be difficult to deal with. Our team has protocols about what kind of behaviour we tolerate from callers; and we have all ended calls when customers become particularly abusive. But our role is to listen and help people talk through their concerns. It can be very upsetting to listen to their stories and their anger.

None of us wants to take this home, and we have various ways of supporting each other. Some of these are formal methods: time out after a particularly difficult call, and standing in for someone, for instance. But the most important support is informal, a team member listening or doing something that makes us laugh and relieves the tension. The thing is we do the same work, we all know what it can be like, so we can help each other out.

As a team leader you can take the lead by showing your support and commitment to the team. Your focus can be on practical action:

◆ Be a team advocate

◆ Keep the team informed of the bigger picture

◆ Encourage development and learning

◆ Integrate new team members

◆ Celebrate success.

Be a team advocate

You should show your support for the team and for team members as individuals.

- ◆ **Support individuals** – Be approachable so that people feel able to discuss their concerns with you. Listen carefully and show that you understand and accept what they are saying. You don't have to agree. Help them to find their own solution.

- ◆ **Support the team** – Work with the team to clarify its concerns, interests and requirements and represent these to the rest of the organisation, where appropriate.

For example, you can be clear about what the team needs from those who supply it with information and other resources, and help to ensure it has the resources it needs.

Make resources available

- ◆ Identify and agree resource requirements with the team.

- ◆ Compare these with resources currently available.

- ◆ Make available resources where you can.

- ◆ Ensure everyone in the team understands the bigger picture – the constraints that the organisation is facing, for instance.

- ◆ Make a case to senior management for any additional resources required.

- ◆ Keep team members informed of the progress of your case.

Keep the team informed of the bigger picture

Represent the organisation to the team so that they know what is happening in the organisation and their industry or business as a whole. Team members ought to understand the context in which they are operating, as this helps them to see the effect of their efforts on the organisation. It also helps them to understand and accept any constraints that they are operating under. A lost contract, for example, may mean a general restriction on resources.

Encourage development and learning

People need to keep developing their skills, knowledge and understanding in order to remain employable. So it is reassuring when we can develop and improve in the workplace. Many organisations recognise the importance of supporting development of their people:

◆ To ensure that they have the skills they need in the future

◆ To demonstrate that they are good employers and can attract and retain good staff.

Even if your organisation has no formal mechanisms for providing development for staff or if your team is made up of people from different organisations, you can show your commitment to self-development and the personal and professional development of others.

Take the development of team members seriously and look for opportunities for them to achieve their development objectives.

Activity

By reading this book you are showing a willingness to develop and improve your skills and performance.

Think about how you can show a commitment to development in your team.

What learning opportunities can you provide to team members?

You may have suggested training or development off the job, for example, computer-based training, flexible, open or distance learning, or attending short courses or events. You may have also recognised that there are opportunities for development on the job in the team:

◆ **Coaching** – encouraging the development of new skills or knowledge by carrying out activities in the team, and giving constructive feedback.

◆ **Mentoring** – encouraging experienced team members to act as an adviser and guide to new or inexperienced colleagues.

◆ **Reviewing activities** – considering what went well, what went wrong, lessons to be learned and where improvements could be made.

- **Giving constructive feedback** on performance.

- **Problem-solving activities** in the team, such as brainstorming and evaluation sessions.

It's well known that people don't retain what they have learned if they don't practise it – if you don't use it, you lose it. So it is important for team members to have opportunities to apply their new skills and thinking to their work.

Integrate new team members

Changes in team membership disrupt the smooth functioning of the team and can make everybody uneasy. It takes time for a new team member to learn how the team works and to feel that he or she fits in. Your role is to support the team so that it is able to welcome a new member, and to give the new person support so that he or she can settle into the team. Don't sit back to let the person learn the ropes in their own time; take an active role to ease the way.

Help new team members to fit in

- Explore the role and functions of the new team member with the team before he or she joins.

- Set short-term realistic objectives with the new person.

- Ask an experienced team member to act as the new person's 'mentor' or 'buddy' and look after them for a few weeks.

- Get the new team member involved in the team's work early on – perhaps by partnering them with someone else.

- Involve other team members in explaining the team's systems and operations and how to use them.

- Make use of the team contract to help new members learn the team rules, how the team works together and what they expect from each other.

- Make time to talk to new members of the team to get to know them and see how they are doing.

- Make it clear that you want to know if the new team member is experiencing any problems so that you can help to resolve them.

- Review progress with the new team member from time to time.

Celebrate success

This means showing the team that you value its efforts and achievements, and that you feel the team is making a difference.

It is important to recognise the effort and work that team members contribute to both working well as a team and achieving their objectives. It can help people's motivation to receive thanks or praise when they have succeeded. But it is curious how often team leaders and managers neglect this aspect of showing support.

We work really hard to meet the impossible targets and no one says a word to show that they care. In fact those targets become the new standard – onwards and upwards to new levels of pressure and stress.

We reached a milestone in the project with a great deal of relief. It was Christmas time and the team leader sent everyone in the team a box of chocolates with a message, saying: 'We got here. Hooray! Thanks for all your hard work this year.' It made a huge difference to the way we were feeling.

You don't have to make grand gestures to celebrate success. Often a simple but sincere 'Thank you' can mean a lot. Think about these:

◆ Bringing in cakes, pizza, strawberries and cream or some other 'treat' to mark an achievement by the team.

◆ Making a point of thanking individuals or the team as a whole in team meetings.

◆ Writing a letter to your boss highlighting the extra effort made by team members to achieve a particular goal, and pinning it up on the notice board.

◆ Sending a card to people at their home thanking them for their contribution to solving a particularly difficult problem.

Activity

What experience do you have of marking successes in your work with teams?

What seems to work best?

Summary

◆ To help your team to perform well, you need to:

❖ Create shared goals

❖ Encourage motivation among team members

❖ Enable team members to take responsibility for their work by involving them in setting and agreeing objectives and planning and controlling their work

❖ Support the team by representing the team, keeping the team informed of organisational developments, encouraging development, integrating new members and celebrating success.

4 Communications

Communicate! 50

Listen 53

Use questions 57

Run effective team meetings 59

Manage the discussion 64

Use technology for communications 69

'Hi Mum, can you look up the number for Mission Control,
I don't appear to have brought it with me!'

Communicate!

Good, open communications are essential to effective teamwork:

◆ Information must flow freely so that everyone is kept fully up to date.

◆ People must feel able to express their opinion and judgement and be confident that the rest of the team is listening and taking account of their views.

◆ It is only through communicating that the team will be able to build its knowledge and understanding.

◆ Good communications are key to developing mutual trust and support in the team.

Communication skills can always be improved.

> Open communications build understanding.

Open communication is a two-way process depending as much on the response of the receiver as in the quality and substance of the message.

The sender decides to send a message to someone, chooses what to say and transmits it to the receiver. The receiver interprets what the person says and chooses how to respond, sending feedback to the sender, indicating how far the receiver understood the message.

There are numerous barriers – physical, psychological and cultural – that can impede effective open communications:

◆ The message may be vague, confusing or without a clear purpose.

◆ The message may not reach the recipient – because of errors or barriers associated with the method used, for example, an inaccurate email address

- ◆ The recipient may:
  - ❖ Not understand the language or the context of the message
  - ❖ Be preoccupied with other matters and ignore the message
  - ❖ Mishear, because of distractions or background noise
  - ❖ Misinterpret the message because of preconceptions and assumptions about the sender's purpose.

Given the possible barriers, it's surprising that people manage to communicate at all. To avoid potential problems in getting your message across, you could use a simple and quick planning tool when you want to communicate.

Planning tool – PACM

Purpose - What do you want to achieve? Why?

Audience - What are the needs, expectations and interests of the people to whom you are communicating?

Contents - What do you need to say in the message?

Method (and Medium) - How will you get your message across?

Your purpose in communicating is to elicit a response from your recipients, so it is very important to think about how your approach affects your audience.

Activity

Run through this planning tool quickly for the next 10 communications you need to make.

Review the results. How far has it improved your communications?

Promoting open communication

Open communication is honest and shows a genuine respect for other people. It involves keeping an open mind in your communications and not clouding your messages with underlying assumptions and attitudes, such as:

◆ 'I haven't really got time to do this.'

◆ 'I don't care what you think about this – I've made up my mind.'

◆ 'I'm in charge of this.'

◆ 'You can't understand the problem.'

Hidden messages like these often undermine communication: people become defensive and unwilling to respond honestly and openly.

Seek to use any of the following approaches in the messages you send:

◆ **Explaining** – this is what I say and here are my reasons

◆ **Exploring** – seeking to find out people's points of view and the reasons for them.

◆ **Exchanging ideas** – avoiding making assumptions to find areas of difference and common ground.

◆ **Testing** – this is what I say, what do you think about it?

◆ **Observing** – this is what the evidence tells me.

These can all contribute to skilful communication where people are willing to put forward their opinions, but are also willing to explore the reasoning and assumptions behind them. They are also genuinely interested to find out other people's perspectives and assumptions. Essential parts of skilful communications are good listening and questioning skills.

Listen

The ability to listen is a fundamental skill, and is especially useful for team leaders and team members. Listening allows us to learn what's happening and consequently improve our decision-making. Listening improves trust and understanding between people; it shows respect to others and helps to build good relationships.

My team members work all over the UK. We use email a lot for straightforward information. But I keep in touch with what's really happening by talking and listening to team members on the phone. It can be time-consuming, but it's important to show the team that I'm interested in their work and in their views.

Most of us who can hear, think we listen all the time; it's a skill we already have – a given. This is doubtless true: we can listen when we want to. But we also tend to be adept at not listening.

The skill of not listening

Most of us learned to ignore the drone of a boring teacher at school, to filter out the chatter on the radio, to steer conversation our way by interrupting, to look as though we're listening while thinking of something completely different.

I know I don't listen well when I'm on the phone and at my computer at the same time. I think I'm so busy that I don't stop to listen. I may be saying the right things, but I'm probably scanning through my unread mail, so I don't really hear what the other person is saying at all.

I realise I often listen in spurts, especially when someone goes off at a tangent and starts giving me the story in endless minute detail. My mind starts to wander.

Do you know how not to listen? Do you ever:	Yes	No
Listen selectively – tuning in and out until you hear something you want to listen to?	☐	☐
Half-listen to the speaker, while thinking about something else?	☐	☐
Make assumptions and jump to conclusions?	☐	☐
Interrupt with your own ideas?	☐	☐

If you answered 'No' to all of these, you are either a paragon or you need to observe yourself when you are listening.

The ability not to listen may be a survival skill in some circumstances. After all, it is exhausting to absorb everything you hear. But there are drawbacks. First there are the consequences of not hearing the message someone is sending, such as:

◆ Losing the opportunity to learn something new

◆ Missing a clue to someone's behaviour

◆ Missing a potential cause of a problem.

Then there are the personal consequences to you and the speaker. By showing someone you don't think highly enough of them to listen to them, you undermine that person. You make it less likely that the person will take the time to talk to you the next time, so the working relationship between you is weakened. In addition you run a real risk of losing their respect.

Activity

Think of a time when you have been sure that someone hasn't been listening to you.

◆ How did you know?

◆ How did it make you feel?

Sometimes it's obvious when someone is not listening:

In meetings with my boss, I can always tell when she stops listening. She starts to fidget and her eyes are drawn to her computer screen. So of course I stop talking. Last time it happened, I put some papers on her desk for her and saw that she was playing solitaire on screen. Obviously I was being very boring or else she has a short attention span.

At other times the signals are less clear:

Our new team leader has been on all the courses and knows how to go through the motions of listening. The body language is right and he makes encouraging noises at the right time, but there's something in his eyes – I'm sure he's miles away.

Most people can detect when you aren't listening to them.

How to listen

The key to listening effectively is to give your attention to the person who is speaking.

The essentials of listening

- ◆ Decide that you want to listen to the person.

- ◆ Get rid of distractions, such as background noise – find a quiet place to talk or put off the conversation until you can do so.

- ◆ Stop what you are doing – if you can't do this, delay the conversation.

- ◆ Put aside your own concerns – stop your mind from running on with its usual background notes.

- ◆ Concentrate on what the person is saying.

- ◆ Give the person time to think about what to say and let them speak.

- ◆ Try to put yourself in the other's shoes – to see things from where they stand.

If you can do these things then it is likely that the person who is speaking will recognise that you are listening. But you can also reinforce the message that you are listening with your body language and what you say. This can be particularly important when you are listening to someone on the telephone, rather than face to face. On the phone you have to use your voice to reassure the person that you are interested to hear what they are saying.

Here are some tips to show people that you are listening and to give them confidence to keep talking.

Show you are listening

◆ Avoid slouching – be alert and relaxed.

◆ Look at the person, make occasional eye contact, but don't stare.

◆ Avoid distracting behaviour, such as fiddling with a pen or doodling.

◆ Use verbal cues to encourage the person to keep talking and reassure the speaker that you are still listening: 'mm-mm', 'ye-es', 'go on'.

◆ Occasionally summarise what the speaker has said to check you understand: 'So he's in Manchester now?'

◆ Use questions to encourage the person to talk and to clarify any points that are unclear.

Many people find that they naturally use some or all of these tips when they are listening. It's important to use them only in support of listening, not as a charade. If you use these tips to show you're listening, when in reality you're planning the evening's entertainment in your mind, the speaker is unlikely to be fooled.

Use questions

You can use questions to encourage people to talk, to explore and find out more. It is useful to consider the effect of your questions on the speaker, as different types of questions tend to lead to particular responses:

Closed questions can often be answered with a short 'yes', 'no', 'don't know' or a specific piece of information. For example:

> 'Did you phone on Thursday?'

> 'Did you enjoy the work?'

> 'When did that happen?'

They tend to close down a conversation.

Open questions help people to talk more or open up. They often start with 'What...?','How...?' or 'Why...?'

> 'What did you enjoy about the work?'

> 'How did you feel about it?'

> 'What happened next?'

> 'Why did that happen?'

Questions starting with 'Why...?' can sometimes sound confrontational, putting someone on the spot. You may want to soften the effect by saying 'Why do you think...?' or 'Tell me about...'

Clarifying questions seek to ensure understanding by exploring in more detail what someone is saying:

> 'Could you explain what you mean...?'

> 'So are you saying that...?'

Hypothetical questions explore options:

> 'How could we...?'

> 'What would happen if we...'

Probing questions seek to find out more to gain more understanding:

> 'Why did you feel she was undermining you?'

'How did you manage to persuade them to support the idea?'

Leading questions suggest a particular answer – one that the questioner wants to hear:

'You do enjoy the work, don't you?'

'You aren't going to do that, are you?'

It is easy to answer 'yes' or 'no', as expected, especially when there is little conviction either way, and much harder to go against the expectation implied in the question. Leading questions don't enable a speaker to be open and honest.

Activity

Practise listening to a friend. Use *The essentials of listening* (page 55) as your starting point, but also draw on the tips to show you are listening.

Afterwards, think about how successful you were:

◆ What worked well?

◆ What would you like to do better next time?

◆ How did you show you were listening?

◆ What kind of questions worked best for you?

Ask your friend for feedback. How far did he or she feel that you were listening?

People often find that really listening to someone is surprisingly hard work. Many find it difficult to stop the constant chatter in their mind and to focus on trying to understand the other person's point of view. Like most skills it takes practice.

Run effective team meetings

Team meetings are where much of the team's work is done. They can be used for getting reactions to events, exchanging ideas and opinions, solving problems, making decisions and agreeing on action.

But many people get a sinking feeling when they contemplate team meetings.

Activity

What tends to happen or has happened in team meetings you've attended that could lead people to regard a team meeting as an event to be endured?

Here are some reasons why team meetings can be ineffective, a waste of time and a sure way to stamp on people's enthusiasm and commitment to the team.

Obstructions to effective meetings

- ◆ There is no agenda or the agenda is ignored.

- ◆ Reports to be discussed in the meeting aren't distributed to members in sufficient time to enable them to prepare for the meeting.

- ◆ Members turn up late or leave early.

- ◆ The person running the meeting inhibits open discussion by rushing through items on the agenda, talking too much and providing too much direction on solutions.

- ◆ Discussions ramble on, deviate from the point and have no clear direction.

- ◆ Some members dominate and do all the talking.

- ◆ Members hold private conversations or side discussions not connected with the agenda.

- ◆ Some members say nothing.

- ◆ Some members undermine the efforts of others – blocking people's contributions and being unhelpfully critical.

These obstructions are a sign of a lack of discipline among the team, poor skills in controlling the meeting and an indication that people do not regard team meetings as useful or productive. If you experience many of these types of behaviour in a team meeting you can probably conclude the team as a whole is not performing well.

> Team meetings should be a positive, motivating experience that reinforces commitment to achieving shared goals through mutual support.

Although the success of team meetings depends on the way everyone participates, as a team leader you can organise and run effective meetings. It takes commitment, planning, ability to manage the running of the meeting, and techniques for managing the discussion.

Commitment to meetings

It can be very useful to agree procedures and codes of conduct for meetings with team members. Such an agreement highlights the importance of meetings to the team and the need for everyone to play a constructive, positive role. It could form part of the team contract.

Meeting rules

Discuss and agree procedures and behaviour in meetings and write these down. You could cover the following aspects:

◆ Preparation

◆ Formation and distribution of an agenda

◆ Role of team leader, facilitator or chairperson

◆ Attendance

◆ Participation

◆ Agreeing action

◆ Record taking

◆ Follow-up after the meeting.

With agreement and commitment from all members to contribute positively to meetings, you can occasionally monitor and review the way the team is working together against what you have agreed, and plan improvements.

Planning and running the meeting

A meeting needs to be planned and organised, by thinking about:

◆ **The purpose of the meeting** as a whole and of the items that need to be raised.

◆ **Attendance** – a team meeting will involve the team, but you may also need to bring in outsiders to advise on some aspects.

◆ **Location** – where to hold the meeting.

◆ **Timing** – duration of the meeting and the amount of time to spend on the separate items.

◆ **Leading the meeting** – this may be the team leader or chairperson but it may be appropriate for those most concerned with a particular item to lead that part of the meeting.

◆ **Record taking** – who will take notes of the meeting and how, and how the notes will be issued and approved.

◆ **Follow up** – what should happen after the meeting.

Meetings are expensive so consider whether a meeting is necessary. If the intention of a meeting is to make sure that everyone is up to date on progress could a report emailed to everyone in the team do just as well? If the intention is solve a problem or make decisions, it may be essential for team members to meet.

If a meeting is necessary, so too is an agenda.

Agenda

The agenda provides the meeting with a purpose, structure and direction. Without an agenda the meeting is in danger of becoming an aimless discussion – a bit of an indulgence for busy people. The agenda can be quite short and informal but it is useful when it:

◆ Outlines items to be discussed

◆ Gives time guidelines

◆ Identifies who is to lead the discussion – especially if different from the chairperson

◆ Identifies any papers that members need to consider for the meeting.

It ought to be possible for team members to contribute to the agenda – they could be invited to submit items or to comment on a draft agenda. This suggests that the agenda usually has to be drawn up, agreed and issued well before the meeting. However, if a meeting has to be called at short notice you can agree the agenda items at the start.

It is helpful to include an occasional agenda item to review the way the team is working together. This can encourage team members to reflect on their behaviour and how this relates to the expectations agreed in the team contract.

Running the meeting

The chairperson may be a facilitator, in which case he or she is impartial and doesn't contribute to decision-making. If the chairperson is also the team leader with overall responsibility for the team's work then he or she can influence the discussion and, where appropriate, take charge.

People generally prefer the chairperson to keep firm control of a meeting so that it can progress successfully. This means making a judgement on how to introduce each item, how to encourage helpful contributions and how to keep the discussion on track.

So the chairperson has to do the following:

◆ Keep in mind the purpose behind each item on the agenda. Is the intention to:

❖ Air different views?

❖ Explore possibilities?

❖ Gather feedback?

❖ Find a solution?

❖ Make a decision?

◆ Be aware of the background to each item.

◆ Consider team members' likely interests in each item, their concerns and reactions:

❖ What do team members expect or need from a discussion of this item?

❖ What are their concerns?

❖   What are the likely reactions from team members?

❖   Who is likely to feel defensive?

◆   Decide when to encourage ideas, when to push for a resolution, when to allow time for further discussion, when to move onto the next agenda item.

◆   Encourage positive and fair participation from team members.

◆   Check understanding, offer suggestions, summarise.

◆   Review the meeting afterwards.

These points all require good communication skills and a good understanding of interpersonal behaviours.

Activity

Consider the last meeting you ran and use this checklist to review what happened.

Did you?	Yes	No
Issue an agreed agenda in good time?	☐	☐
Inform all participants of its location, start time and duration?	☐	☐
Start on time?	☐	☐
Refer to notes from the previous meeting?	☐	☐
Use the agenda during the meeting?	☐	☐
Appoint someone to keep a record?	☐	☐
Introduce each item and explain what had to be achieved in the meeting?	☐	☐
Listen carefully to contributions?	☐	☐
Keep a focus on the purpose of each agenda item?	☐	☐
Encourage equal and fair participation from everyone?	☐	☐
Ask for clarification when appropriate?	☐	☐
Summarise the discussion and any action agreed?	☐	☐
Maintain a good pace through the items on the agenda?	☐	☐
Thank participants for their contributions?	☐	☐
End the meeting on time?	☐	☐

Manage the discussion

You can develop your chairing skills by practising them, reflecting on what happens in your meetings and what you can do differently next time. You can also use a range of techniques or activities to manage the discussion and control participation from people.

A team meeting ought to be an opportunity to voice and explore different opinions, to argue a case and disagree. The benefits of teamwork arise from the team's ability to consider different ideas and make an informed judgement on the ones that will be most effective.

You can encourage team members to express ideas, and explore different opinions. However, you have to do this sensitively, and judge when to move the discussion on towards agreement. One way of doing this is to manage the flow of the meeting by imposing some structure on the discussions.

Ideas for managing contributions

◆ Go round each team member in turn and ask for their ideas, opinions or judgment. This is useful when there are dominant and reticent members.

◆ Split the team into small groups of two or three people and ask them to consider an issue for several minutes and then report back to the full group in turn. Again this is useful to give everyone a chance to contribute equally.

◆ Use the problem-solving and decision-making techniques that are described later in this book to enable team members to concentrate on a particular way of thinking, whether this means being creative or analytical.

◆ Run a session with team members to consider how the way they respond to suggestions or ideas affects the flow of the discussion. For example:

Comment	Response
Why don't we...	No, but...
	Yes, and we could...
	Yes, how do you think we could ...?
	That won't work because...

◆ Use the six hats thinking technique.

Six hats thinking

The six hats thinking technique was devised by Edward de Bono, a renowned expert in lateral and creative thinking. This technique show that there are different types of thinking and allows the team to adopt a particular type of thinking at different times. This promotes clarity and minimises confusion and contradictions.

The six hats

Hat colour	Used for:
Blue	Controlling which hat is used at any time
White	Expressing facts and evidence
Green	Being creative and generating ideas
Yellow	Exploring positive aspects of a situation; useful for evaluating ideas
Black	Exploring the negative aspects of a situation; useful for evaluating ideas
Red	Exploring feelings, emotion and intuition about a situation

There are two main ways of using the six hats:

◆ Ask each team member to adopt a particular coloured hat and contribute to the discussion from that perspective. You can also ask people to swap hats, for example:

'John, will you wear the red hat for a minute... and Rebecca, if you would put on the white hat?'

◆ Ask everyone in the team to adopt the same colour hat at any one time, for example:

'Let's all put on the black hat and think about why this idea won't work.'

Here are some ideas for using the six hats thinking technique.

Run a six hats thinking session

◆ At first it can feel awkward to use the six hats technique, so it is useful to treat the six hats as a game.

◆ Find different coloured hats that people can put on – they could be paper hats, for example.

- Display a list of the different coloured hats and what each one means on a flipchart when people are unfamiliar with the technique.

- Refer to the six hats by colour so that people learn to connect the colour to the style of thinking.

- Wear the blue hat to control proceedings, but be prepared to change hats if you are contributing. For example, tell the team that you are taking off the blue hat and putting on the white hat to give some factual information.

- Limit the length of the session and review the results of the discussion and the effectiveness of the technique.

Handling difficult situations

You are likely to encounter some or all of the following when you run meetings:

- Hidden agendas or unspoken intentions
- Talkers
- The meeting seems stuck
- Side discussions
- Arguments.

Here are some ideas on how to deal with them.

Hidden agendas

Look out for any hidden agendas that may be influencing apparently rational arguments. For example:

- Are some team members in competition?
- Is someone engaging in point scoring or in undermining or attacking another?
- Is someone feeling that their work is being criticised?
- Is someone feeling defensive?

You can do this by listening not just to what is being said but to the body language and to the emotion that seems to be behind it.

You have several options:

◆ Remind people of the objective of the discussion.

◆ Ignore it and move on – but be aware that the underlying emotions may still influence the debate.

◆ Bring the hidden agenda out into the open. For example: 'Do you have another concern that you'd like to raise here?'

◆ Acknowledge that people have other concerns, but ask them to put them to one side, unless they are relevant to the objective of the discussion.

Talkers

Some people have a lot to say; they may simply be enthusiastic or knowledgeable. Thank them for their contribution, say that the meeting should hear what others have to say and ask another person for their views. Consider whether talkers always seem to take centre stage whatever the issue or only on certain issues that particularly interest or concern them. You may decide to give constructive feedback to a persistent talker in private after a meeting.

A stuck meeting

Occasional silence may be a sign that people are thinking, absorbing the implications of an option. But when no one seems to have anything to say you could try these techniques for restarting the discussion:

◆ Summarise what has been said so far and outline what still needs to be done.

◆ Ask a particular team member – perhaps a natural talker – to comment on progress so far and how they would move on.

◆ Make a suggestion – maybe a controversial one – of a way forward and ask for reactions.

Side discussions

These are distracting and can be discourteous to the rest of the meeting. It's important to bring the meeting back together:

◆ Ask one of the people in the side discussion for their views – summarising the issue for them if appropriate, so that you aren't seen as undermining them.

Arguments

These can be useful, and they can become heated when people feel passionate about their work. They can also become hurtful and personal. You need to keep the temperature down:

◆ Remind people to focus on what is being said.

◆ Concentrate attention on the issues, not on personalities.

◆ Remind people, if necessary, to avoid getting personal.

◆ Highlight areas where there is agreement.

◆ Protect team members from personal attack.

◆ Summarise the main arguments and move on to find a way forward.

Activity

Think about the different techniques and suggestions described here and identify those that you may find useful in future.

In particular, plan to use activities to structure the discussion.

Reflect on what happens when you use a particular technique.

◆ How well did it work?

◆ What could you have done differently?

◆ How would you use it in future?

This section has focused on meetings and discussions that people attend in person. However, when team members don't work in the same location or work shifts, such meetings can be difficult to arrange. In this case you could make use of technological methods for holding meetings and discussions.

Use technology for communications

Face-to-face discussions and meetings can be difficult or impossible to arrange when team members are dispersed. With the aid of information and communications technology, there are several technological methods that teams can use:

◆ Email

◆ Teleconferencing

◆ Videoconferencing

◆ Web-based 'discussion forums'.

Each has advantages and disadvantages and some of these methods are used by teams that work in the same location. But the fact that the message is mediated through technology means that it is important to plan and give consideration to their use.

> Technology makes communicating at a distance possible. But it is still a barrier.

Email

Is there anyone in business who doesn't use email? It is an excellent tool for communicating, especially with people who work at a distance from each other. You can:

◆ Send a message quickly.

◆ Send it to a group of people at the same time.

◆ Use the email software to organise and store your messages and keep track of the flow of information about a subject.

◆ Get a quick response to a message.

However, its popularity brings with it some difficulties, apart from ubiquitous junk emails:

If you need something urgently, don't email me because I get over 200 messages a day – I pick and choose the ones I read. Phone my mobile and leave a message or text me.

Fibreoptics engineer

I was told the people at an organisation I worked with were perfectly happy using email, but I ended up giving tutorials over the phone about how to attach files properly.

Development consultant

Email speeds everything up. I left it to the last minute before sending the report because I really needed that last minute. What I didn't allow for was the server going down so in the end the report didn't get sent in time. The technology is fantastic and we depend on it. But it does let you down.

Team leader, cosmetics company

Guidelines for using email

◆ Think about who really needs to receive the email, rather than sending all messages to everyone in the team.

◆ Put a clear meaningful title into the subject box so that people can keep track of their emails by the subject heading.

◆ Keep the message short, as you would a letter. Send long documents as attachments.

◆ For attachments, use the 'add attachment' button and browse. Dragging a file into the attachment box can corrupt the file.

Emails can be the main form of communication when the team is dispersed. Use the steps for planning communications to get your message across. In addition, it is important to think about tone.

Tone

You can communicate your mood and attitude in just a few written words on an email, and a tone that clashes with the contents of a message can easily undermine its purpose.

Do you want your team members to sense that you are being friendly? Concerned? Professional? Irritated? Do you want them to be motivated, encouraged, enthusiastic? Do you want them to feel you are giving them an order or a request? Do you want them to feel valued and respected?

Busy people often rely heavily on emails and send short, terse messages to each other. But when team members work apart, or meet only rarely, the tone of an email can have a significant effect on them.

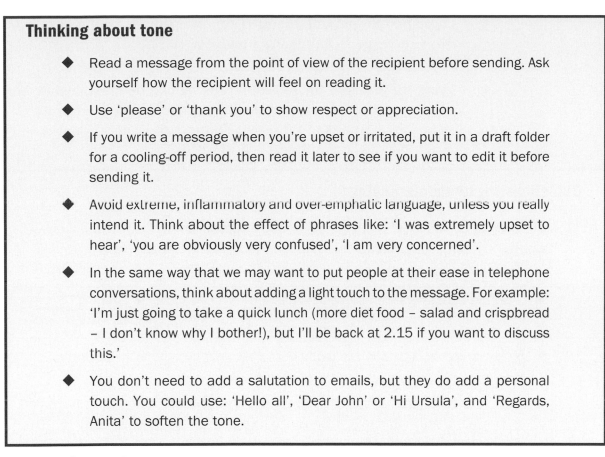

Thinking about tone

◆ Read a message from the point of view of the recipient before sending. Ask yourself how the recipient will feel on reading it.

◆ Use 'please' or 'thank you' to show respect or appreciation.

◆ If you write a message when you're upset or irritated, put it in a draft folder for a cooling-off period, then read it later to see if you want to edit it before sending it.

◆ Avoid extreme, inflammatory and over-emphatic language, unless you really intend it. Think about the effect of phrases like: 'I was extremely upset to hear', 'you are obviously very confused', 'I am very concerned'.

◆ In the same way that we may want to put people at their ease in telephone conversations, think about adding a light touch to the message. For example: 'I'm just going to take a quick lunch (more diet food – salad and crispbread – I don't know why I bother!), but I'll be back at 2.15 if you want to discuss this.'

◆ You don't need to add a salutation to emails, but they do add a personal touch. You could use: 'Hello all', 'Dear John' or 'Hi Ursula', and 'Regards, Anita' to soften the tone.

Teleconferencing

Teleconferencing allows a group of people to talk to each other via the telephone or Internet. It can be used to follow up on progress or to have a quick consultation on an issue that all participants are familiar with. It is best used by people who know each other quite well, but is not so useful for detailed consultations.

The success of a teleconference can depend on how much participants trust each other and are prepared to speak honestly and openly. This is because participants are not able to observe each other's body language, and have to listen to the tone, volume and speed of the voice in order to understand how someone is feeling. Although this is quite possible in a telephone conversation between two people, it can be confusing when there are multiple voices.

Teleconferences can take place on multi-party telephone lines or via the Internet, and requires suitable equipment.

- Three people can talk together on an ordinary phone line. But when more participants are involved, one needs to have teleconferencing equipment.

- Using the Internet for teleconferencing can be inexpensive, but all users need to have, and be able to use, suitable equipment, including a broadband Internet connection, a good quality computer, with a soundcard, and headphones.

Guidelines for teleconferencing

A chairperson or moderator must control the conference carefully.

- Teleconferencing requires a lot of concentration and careful listening. Keep it as short as possible.

- Test the equipment with participants before the scheduled conference.

- Do a sound check with each person when they come on line.

- When everyone is present, go round each participant by name, asking for a response, so that everyone knows who is there and hears the person's voice.

- Explain the purpose of the conference and how you intend to run it. For example, do you intend to go round each participant in a particular order to hear everyone's contribution? This can overcome a common problem participants have in not knowing when they can speak.

- Explain the basic rules for taking part:

  ❖ Don't interrupt another person when he or she is speaking.

  ❖ Let the moderator call on people in turn to make a contribution.

  ❖ When you want to make a contribution, and have not been called, wait for a pause and ask the moderator, giving your name first.

- Summarise regularly during the conference, and identify any action that needs to be agreed.

- Occasionally open the discussion by asking if someone wants to add anything.

- Use closed questions to seek agreement.

- At the end summarise the outcomes of the conference and the action agreed and thank participants for attending.

Videoconferencing

Videoconferencing involves audio and video. All participants can see and hear each other. This has obvious benefits over teleconferencing, but seeing participants on screen is clearly not the same as seeing them face to face. The technology can still get in the way.

Videoconferencing usually takes place in special suite, and technicians set up and test the equipment. People increasingly talk about using 'webcams' (cameras that record pictures and broadcast them live on the Internet) for web-based videoconferencing. Some companies offer this for up to four participants. Their success seems to depend on high powered computers and a high bandwidth connection, together with a good light source directed at the person being videoed.

Guidelines for using videoconferencing

As with other conferencing methods, videoconferencing needs a chairperson or moderator who can manage the flow and discussion of a face-to-face meeting:

◆ Book a session for the videoconference, making sure all participants can attend the videoconference facilities at their location.

◆ Avoid wearing patterned, black or white clothes – they tend to pixellate on screen.

◆ Arrive early so the technicians can set up the camera to suit you.

◆ Speak to the camera – perhaps a little more deliberately or slowly than you normally do.

◆ Welcome people to the conference, introduce them if necessary, and check sound and video quality.

◆ Explain how you plan to run the videoconference, how to use the equipment (if necessary) and ask participants to:

❖ Allow one person to speak at a time

❖ Avoid interrupting a speaker as this cuts out the other person's voice

❖ Be prepared for a time delay between the video and audio transmission

❖ Use the mute button if you are going to cough or if you need to talk off camera.

Web-based discussion forums

A web-based conference or discussion forum can take place over time. It is useful for a team that wants to explore an issue in depth and see how ideas developed. Using a forum is easy for anyone who uses emails, but many people are wary at first. Participants log on to a private forum on a website. They can start a discussion by posting a message or they can respond to another person's post. A moderator oversees the progress of the discussion.

Guidelines for moderating a web-based forum

◆ Give an agenda, objectives and duration of the forum at the start of the page.

◆ Make sure everyone knows who the participants are and what your role is.

◆ Provide help and reassurance to people unfamiliar with the technology.

◆ Be clear about acceptable language and behaviour, for example, does spelling matter if the meaning is clear? Explain your role in editing or deleting posts where necessary.

◆ Encourage people to respond to posts by replying, rather than by starting a new post. This enables everyone to follow the thread of the discussion.

◆ Be prepared to:

   ❖ Remind participants of the objectives of the forum if the discussion deviates from the point and

   ❖ Make controversial comments or suggestions to stimulate responses.

◆ Regularly provide a summary and any agreed action so this can be started before the forum comes to an end.

Activity

Think about the technological methods for communicating explored in this section. If your team is dispersed you may rely on some of these methods.

◆ Which are or could be useful tools for your team to use?

◆ Find out more about how you and team members could access appropriate technologies – you could consult experts or colleagues in your organisation who have experience of these.

◆ Consider practising different methods. Expect there to be difficulties in using the technology at first.

◆ Consider discussing and agreeing with your team codes of conduct for using particular technological methods of communication. You could incorporate agreements into the team contract.

Teams that regularly make use of any of these technological methods, usually overcome the technological barriers to communication through practice and familiarity.

Summary

◆ Good, open communications build understanding.

◆ Plan two-way communications by thinking about purpose, audience, contents and method.

◆ Listening is an essential communication skill, and can always be improved. Give the other person your full attention and encourage them to talk.

◆ You can use questions to encourage people to talk, to explore what they are saying and to find out more. Open questions that ask people to talk more and open up are particularly useful.

◆ Team meetings are where much of the team's work is done. They ought to be productive and enjoyable.

◆ Poor team meetings undermine everyone and are a sign of a lack of discipline among the team and poor skills in controlling the meeting.

◆ Meetings need to be well-planned in terms of logistics and agenda.

◆ To achieve the aims of the meeting, the person who runs it must be able to:

  ❖ Control the flow of the meeting

  ❖ Encourage participation from everyone

  ❖ Manage the discussion

  ❖ Handle awkward or difficult situations.

◆ Technological methods are available that enable a dispersed team to communicate. These include email, teleconferencing, videoconferencing and web-based discussions. The barriers associated with the technology can be overcome, especially with practice.

5 Team relationships

Build trust 77

Give and take feedback 82

Deal with conflict 86

Focus on the stakeholders 89

It was around this moment that Al wondered whether he'd been wise
to play that practical joke on his leading partner before the climb

Build trust

Team members need to build productive working relationships that are built on trust if they are to work together as an effective team.

Open communications are important in developing relationships. But so too is trust. We'll start by looking at how you can take the lead in building trust and support

An effective team has two key characteristics:

◆ Team members work together in a supportive way.

◆ Team members work to achieve shared, common goals.

These characteristics depend on trust.

◆ Team members need to be able to trust one another. This means that they have confidence and are able to rely on someone's abilities and good personal qualities, such as honesty and being fair.

◆ Team members must also be trustworthy, i.e. deserving trust. They have to be dependable, honest and authentic.

Trust has to be earned by:

◆ Communicating openly

◆ Demonstrating that you trust others

◆ Being trustworthy.

> It is up to you to take the lead in building trust.

Communicating openly

The chapter on Communications gave ideas about communicating effectively and openly. But a valuable approach for considering how open you are in your relationships with other people, and the effect this can have on trust, is the Johari window.

Johari window

The Johari window is so-named after Joe Luft and Harry Ingham, the American theorists who developed it. Our personality is made up from a collection of assumptions, attitudes, beliefs, feelings, emotions, experiences and motivations – and aspects of our personality come into play in our team relationships. The Johari window suggests that in our interactions with other people aspects of our personality can be placed into one of four windows:

◆ **Open** – these are attitudes and feelings that we know about and that are known to others

◆ **Blind** – these are aspects of out personality that others know about us, but we don't know ourselves

◆ **Hidden** – these are parts of our personality that we understand about ourselves, but keep hidden from other people

◆ **Unknown** – aspects of our personality that we don't know about and that are not apparent to other people. However, they may influence our behaviour.

Look at the following diagram:

The Johari window

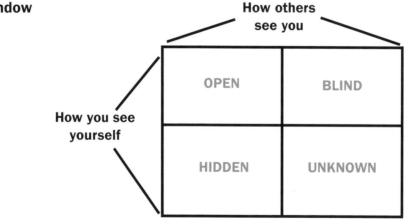

On first meeting someone the open window is small. You reveal little about yourself and there is little trust.

If you want to get to know someone, you have to be prepared to take a risk by showing trust and disclosing more about yourself. This increases the size of the open window and decreases the hidden window. By showing you are willing to take the first step and trust the person you encourage them to reciprocate, and mutual trust starts to develop. As trust develops you gain confidence in the other person and feel able to ask them for feedback to increase the open window further and decrease the blind window:

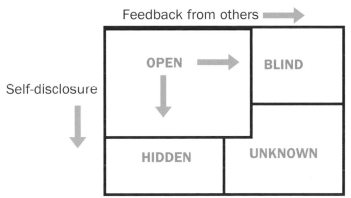

By increasing the open window you are increasing your readiness and openness in giving and receiving information. You show yourself to be able to act with honesty in your relationships.

Consider a different experience when you first meet someone. You hold back from giving information about yourself, waiting to see if you are prepared to commit to a relationship with them. Instead you ask questions, encouraging them to disclose aspects of their personality. The other person may sense they are being tested, and feel disconcerted when you fail to reciprocate. This is unlikely to build trust.

Using the Johari window

You can use the concept of the Johari window to increase the trust and understanding in your team relationships:

◆ Take the first step and let team members know more about what you are like as a person. This in turn encourages them to feel more confident about revealing aspects of themselves.

◆ You don't have to talk about your personal life – you can keep that private while building trust in the team.

◆ One approach is to concentrate on what interests all parties: the team's tasks and goals and how to achieve them.

◆ Be honest and open about your views in respect of the team's goals and work.

◆ Encourage feedback from others to help reveal aspects of your behaviour that you aren't aware of (the blind window).

Think about formal and informal ways of getting to know your team and help them get to know you. This can help build trust in the team.

Bear in mind that your team members may feel at a disadvantage: even though you may not know team members personally, you probably know something of them from job applications, curriculum vitae, appraisals and performance reviews.

Trusting others

Another approach to building trust, especially when you have responsibility for the work of the team, is to release some control and show trust. Control and trust are related. The more you are able to trust someone to do a particular task the more control you can give to them.

Release control; show trust

When you give other people control of a task it is essential that the person who controls the task is successful, and that your trust is seen to be well-placed.

You can minimise the risks of releasing control by using an appropriate leadership style. We looked at leadership style in Chapter 3 on Team performance.

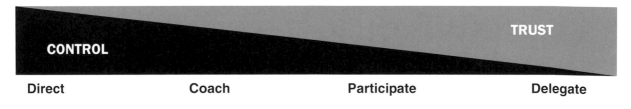

| Direct | Coach | Participate | Delegate |

This shows four main styles that you can use with the team and how they each relate to levels of control and trust.

Being trustworthy

Team members will take the lead from you. You will be seen as a role model and will help to establish the team culture: the way it works and the standards of behaviour that become the norm. So it is important to inspire confidence and trust through the way you behave.

Activity

Think about a manager or leader whom you trust and why you think they are trustworthy. Describe what they do that inspires your confidence in them.

Look at the personal behaviours listed below. How far do you agree with these? Are there others you think are important? Add these to the list.

Rate yourself against your list of personal behaviours for being trustworthy. In what areas do you think you could make improvements?

Personal behaviours to inspire trust

◆ Treat people fairly.

◆ Show you value and respect them.

◆ Be clear about your expectations and the reasons for them.

◆ Do what you say you are going to do.

◆ Make sure the information you give is accurate and up to date.

◆ When you make a mistake, admit it readily and rectify it as soon as you can.

◆ Communicate openly and honestly.

◆ Show you are interested in your team and are able to respond to their needs.

◆ Show that you are personally competent.

◆ Demonstrate good self-management skills, for example, managing workload, controlling stress, maintaining a good work-life balance.

◆ Demonstrate a commitment to learning and improving.

Even the best leaders are likely to fall short from time to time in demonstrating trustworthy behaviour. But in the spirit of learning and development, we can all improve if we choose to do so.

Give and take feedback

If no one tells you when you're doing something well, or when you're making a mess of something, how will you find out? It is important to know how to give constructive feedback and how to make positive use of feedback that you receive.

I am a contractor and work for myself so I don't get feedback. If I don't get a contract I've tendered for no one ever tells me whether I was close or miles off. So I don't know how to improve my chances the next tender I put in. I have to depend on my own assessment and judgement, and it's not easy.

Feedback is a great opportunity to learn and learn quickly, and I'd welcome it. Well, I'd welcome it if it is given in the right spirit – to help me to improve.

Feedback can be highly valuable. It can give you information about your behaviour and performance that otherwise you may struggle to learn. But, to be effective, it is best given in a constructive manner.

Give constructive feedback

Your aims in giving feedback are to:

◆ Help someone improve his or her performance

◆ Offer someone praise.

If your intention is to criticise, vent anger, frustration or irritation, then you won't be giving constructive feedback. You'll be communicating your emotions, rather than a desire to help someone improve. So in this situation it is better not to attempt it.

You are likely to have formal opportunities to give feedback. For example, during 360° appraisals, performance reviews or other review sessions. You may also have informal opportunities, for example, after someone has done a particular task.

To give someone constructive feedback think about how your approach, your tone of voice and the language you use will affect the other person's willingness to be receptive and use your feedback in a positive way. Put yourself in their position, think about what you know of his or her personality and plan your feedback accordingly.

How to give constructive feedback

◆ Give feedback soon after an event so that it is clear in the person's mind.

◆ Give feedback in private so that the person can concentrate on what you say and is not distracted.

◆ Base feedback on observation and/or evidence so that the other person can consider the same facts.

◆ Be specific, be clear, be relevant. Vague concerns, poorly expressed will only confuse.

◆ Focus on a few key issues. Don't overwhelm people with too many; they are more likely to feel able to respond positively to one or two, than to five or six.

◆ Comment on the work, behaviour or performance, not personal qualities or personality.

◆ Focus on things that the person can change, ignore those they can't change.

◆ Point out positive aspects of the work, behaviour or performance so that the person can be reassured that what they did had some good points.

◆ Give the person time to ask questions and absorb what you are saying.

◆ Invite the person to respond and explore the effects of the work, behaviour or performance together and what could be done differently.

◆ Suggest ideas that the person might like to consider to improve performance next time.

◆ Finish on a positive, optimistic note.

Activity

Think about how you give feedback.

◆ Go through the tips above and tick those that you already use regularly.

◆ Highlight those you haven't used, but that you think might be useful in future.

◆ Plan to use these the next time you give feedback.

◆ Check how well you give feedback by asking the recipient for feedback on your performance. You could ask the person how he or she feels at the end of the feedback session, and how you could improve on your approach.

Receiving feedback

If you receive feedback that is given honestly and sensitively, that has your interests in mind and that draws on the ideas given here, then you can easily benefit from it.

It is worth asking for feedback from your fellow team members in order to develop your skills.

Taking feedback from someone

◆ Bear in mind that the person may be uncomfortable giving feedback.

◆ Use questions to encourage the person to express opinions.

◆ Focus on specific aspects of your work, behaviour or performance that you want information about.

◆ Listen carefully to what the other person says and ask for clarification if something is not clear to you.

◆ Be open-minded when receiving feedback. Don't react defensively to criticism. It may be valid.

◆ Thank the person for the feedback.

If you distrust the motives of someone who is giving feedback, for example if you suspect they are trying to undermine or belittle you, then you are unlikely to respond positively to what they have to say.

But bear in mind that people do not always have the skills and the sensitivity to give feedback in a constructive manner. They may appear to be accusing or critical; they may be blunt; they may not be clear or specific about what they think you did; they may ramble and not get to the point.

When this happens your initial reaction may be defensive – you may feel under attack. However, you can choose how to respond to such an approach. You can decide to listen carefully and find out whether you can learn from what the person has to say.

Plain speaking and planning

I work in a small firm and my boss is the owner of the company. He is abrasive and forthright, and you can always trust him to speak his mind.

Last week he told me, in between swearing, that it had taken me three times longer than he'd budgeted for me to do a job. He wanted to know why it had taken so ******* long. I was taken aback; I thought the job had gone well.

We talked about what I'd done and he told me how he'd have done it – the right way, he said. As we talked, it became clear that I hadn't properly planned how to do the job, and that was probably why it took so long. We agreed that I could do with improving my planning and that next time, I'll okay my plans with him to make sure I'm doing it in the best way.

Feedback in teams

As a team leader you can encourage people to give and take feedback constructively and frequently. Here are some ideas:

◆ Be a role model in both the way you give feedback and in the way you seek it out and receive it.

◆ Lead a session with the team on the value of feedback and how best to give and receive it.

◆ Incorporate feedback into your team charter.

◆ Make feedback a normal part of the work of the team – use questionnaires at the end of team meetings, for example.

◆ Build feedback into your review sessions.

Deal with conflict

Disagreements about how to work together and how to achieve common goals are a necessary and positive part of working in a creative dynamic team. When they are openly expressed and resolved, these conflicts can help the team sort out the best way forward and can lead to better decisions.

In fact, if team members agree on most things without much discussion the team may be guilty of 'groupthink' – where conformity to the team becomes the most valued part of being a team member.

Conflict between team members arises when they are in disagreement with each other and their attitudes, priorities, values or ways of working clash. Such conflict can become very personal, with stand up arguments or an undercurrent of ill-will and antagonism between both parties. In such a situation it can be destructive.

It can divide the team, create an uncomfortable atmosphere and undermine the team's ability to work effectively to meet its objectives.

Sources and signs of conflict

Conflict can occur because of:

◆   Personality differences

◆   Different beliefs and values

◆   A long-held grievance that has never been resolved

◆   A battle for influence or power.

When people are working closely to achieve common goals and experience time or work pressures, destructive conflict can arise.

Signs of conflict may include:

◆   Aggressive behaviour

◆   Destructive or hurtful criticism

◆   Refusal to cooperate

◆   Lack of interest in work.

Approaches to dealing with conflict

Although you can't force people to overcome their differences, your concern for getting the job done and for the overall atmosphere in the team means that you can't ignore conflict.

> In 1976, K.W. Thomas described five different approaches to dealing with conflict (*Handbook of Industrial and Organizational Psychology*, Rand McNally). He suggested that the different styles showed how concerned people were in meeting their own needs and the needs of other people.

These approaches to dealing with conflict are:

◆ **Avoidance** – you avoid each other. This suggests a low concern with meeting both your own needs and those of the other person.

◆ **Accommodation** – apologising and standing down from your own position. This suggests a low concern with meeting your own needs and a high concern with the other person's.

◆ **Confrontation** – demanding apologies and some kind of recompense. This suggests a high concern with meeting your own needs and a low concern with the other person's.

◆ **Compromise** – finding a way for you both to save face. This bargaining position shows a moderate concern with meeting both your needs and the other person's.

◆ **Collaboration** – focusing on joint problem-solving. This approach shows a high concern for both your needs and the other person's

The first three approaches may be short-term solutions, but they don't help to solve the conflict in the long term; indeed they may build resentment when one person feels he or she has lost out to the other.

Compromise may be acceptable. This depends on bargaining and can lead to a win-win situation. But it is also possible that both parties may feel that they have lost.

Where people have to work together, a more successful approach is to encourage those involved to collaborate in joint problem-solving.

Reflect on your experiences of conflict in the workplace.

◆ Briefly describe the situation.

◆ Explain the effect this was having on other people.

◆ Describe how the conflict was tackled.

◆ What happened as a result?

◆ How would you deal with the conflict now?

You can take on the role of a mediator to encourage joint problem-solving, but bear in mind that your ability to deal successfully with conflict among team members will depend on how much they trust you.

Ideas for resolving conflict through problem-solving

◆ Allow people some time and distance from each other to get over the immediate hurt and lost tempers.

◆ Encourage both parties to agree to meet with the aim of resolving their differences and finding a way forward.

◆ Use a step-by-step approach to problem-solving in order to explore the conflict.

◆ Focus on the facts and be impartial.

◆ Encourage both parties to look at what caused the conflict, identify options for resolving it and the pros and cons of each option.

◆ Encourage each person to express their opinions and feelings openly.

◆ Encourage each person to listen to the other's views and respond in a non-defensive manner.

◆ Help people to see the situation from the other person's point of view.

◆ Provide regular impartial summaries of the discussion.

◆ Encourage each person to reach an agreed solution.

Focus on the stakeholders

The last part of the chapter goes outside the team to relationships with stakeholders. This is important – the team must not become so self-contained that it forgets the people outside the team who have an interest or stake in its performance.

A danger for a team with a strong team spirit is that it becomes insular, looking exclusively at the concerns and interests of the team, and disregarding the world outside. There may be a tendency for an 'us versus them' attitude when the team bolsters itself at the expense of the people outside the team.

A useful way to counter this is to be constantly aware of your stakeholders.

> Stakeholders are the people and the groups who have an interest or a stake in what you do.

The stakeholder concept

No organisation can survive without customers, so it must meet their needs. It must also serve the interests of its owners or shareholders. Customers and owners may be the organisation's two most important stakeholders. But the organisation influences and is affected by a wider range of groups: the employees, suppliers, subcontractors, local communities, government, Inland Revenue, regulators. All these are stakeholders and have their own interests in and ability to influence the activities and performance of the organisation.

It is important to manage stakeholder groups, understanding their needs and communicating how the organisation's plans will meet those needs.

The idea of stakeholders can be used at any level of the organisation, including individual and team level. Your team's stakeholders have a role to play in its success so you need to work with them. But first you have to understand them.

Stakeholder analysis

With your team:

◆ Identify the team's stakeholders

◆ Consider their main expectations and requirements. Your team may have a good understanding of these, or you may need to do some research, perhaps by talking to them

◆ Assess the influence or power of each group

◆ Identify what your team does and what it needs to do to meet the stakeholder needs.

Identify the team's stakeholders

The team's stakeholders are all the people and groups that have an interest in, are influenced by or can influence the work of the team. Your team's key stakeholders will be its suppliers and customers.

Suppliers are the people and groups that provide your team with the products and services it needs to perform and meet its objectives. They may be external and/or internal:

◆ External suppliers include subcontractors, and suppliers of machinery, equipment and services

◆ Internal suppliers may include managers who provide your team with information, expertise, finance, e.g. a personnel department that supplies training services to your team.

Customers are the people and groups that receive the outputs from your team – its products and services. Again, they may be external and/or internal:

◆ External customers are those firms, organisations or members of the general public who buy or use the team's services and products.

◆ Internal customers are the people or groups inside the organisation to whom you supply products and services.

You may also have other key stakeholders, such as the local community or regulators. Consider the stakeholders in the following case.

The small boatyard team in a marina is responsible for lifting boats, laying them up in the yard and launching them, and for managing the general condition of the yard. The team identified its key stakeholders as follows:

External customers:

◆ **Berthholders** want their boats hauled and laid up in the winter and relaunched in the spring

◆ **Visiting boat owners** want their boats stored afloat in the marina or ashore

Internal customers:

◆ **Maintenance and repair team** requires boats to be moved and laid up

◆ **The management team** wants regular reports of boat movements

◆ **Finance** wants details of boats and customers for billing purposes

External suppliers:

◆ **Engineering company** provides specialist services to maintain the boat moving plant

◆ **Waste disposal companies** provide a variety of refuse services

◆ **Fuel supplier** brings a regular tanker of diesel for plant and for the marina

Internal suppliers:

◆ **Steel fabrication department** makes boat cradles for storage of boats

◆ **Management team** supplies information about company strategy, costing, events, news

Local community:

◆ **Local residents**, walkers, birdwatchers, anglers all have an interest in the condition of the site.

Consider stakeholders' expectations

All your stakeholders will have requirements that they expect your team to meet. The team's success in meeting these expectations will affect their level of satisfaction with your team. It is highly likely that you have to balance competing expectations. Look at the different requirements on the boatyard team for example.

Here are the expectations of some of the boatyard team's key stakeholders:

Stakeholder	Main expectations
Berthholders	To be able to book in for a haul out and launch at short notice
	To be hauled and launched safely on date agreed
	To receive favourable terms
	To be informed of any deals
	To be able to use marina facilities at all times
	To be assured of security of site
Visiting boat owners	To be able to book a haul out and launch at reasonable notice
	To be hauled and launched safely on date agreed
	To be able to use the marina facilities when on site
Maintenance & repair team	To have boats moved safely on demand

You can see that there are competing demands here: the boatyard team can't meet the needs of the maintenance and repair team at all times while also keeping to its agreed schedule for external customers.

It is important to work out how best to meet the different needs.

Assess the influence of stakeholders

You are likely to find that some stakeholder groups have more power and influence than others. Many people would argue that customers should have the most power, because without customers there is no organisation and no team.

Although this is so, in practice the customers' power can be low in comparison to other groups' power or influence. Perhaps this is because customers rarely have a direct or immediate impact on a team's work. In contrast, senior managers, for example, can have an immediate effect on the work of a team.

Decide how to meet different needs

You need to decide how to deal with the different needs and how far to take account of the stakeholders' power and influence.

Look again at the boatyard team's work:

The maintenance and repair team are on the spot and are able to exert influence on the boatyard team, so that their needs are prioritised. This often means that the boat moving schedule is disrupted, boats don't get moved at the agreed time and customers become frustrated.

The boatyard team leader has to balance the different needs, especially during busy months. He sets time aside for unscheduled boat movements and gives external customers a span of time during which boat will be launched, rather than a specific time. This compromise usually works, although the senior management team complain about what they see as a 'relaxed' schedule.

Above all, he makes sure that his team communicates well with customers, so that they know what is happening and why. This promotes customer goodwill, which helps to offset their potential disappointment.

Keeping your stakeholders informed of your team's activities is clearly important. It is also useful to ask for feedback from them and find out what they most value from your team, and how they feel you can meet their needs. Think about what opportunities your team has for communicating with its stakeholders.

Activity

Carry out a stakeholder analysis with your team. You may find it helpful to use a chart with the following headings:

Stakeholder	Main expectations	Power/influence (high, medium, low)	Team's response

Discuss with your team how best to manage the different stakeholders and how to ensure the team keeps open regular communication with them. For example:

◆ Hold regular meetings with internal stakeholders

◆ Issue a regular report or newsletter for particular groups of stakeholders

◆ Use questionnaires to find out stakeholders' expectations and how well you are meeting them.

Summary

◆ In order to work supportively towards shared goals, team members need to trust each other.

◆ You can take the lead in building trust by communicating openly in developing relationships with team members, demonstrating that you trust team members by giving them control over their work and showing that you are personally trustworthy.

◆ The purpose of giving feedback is to help people to improve their performance or offer someone praise so it is important to give constructive feedback.

◆ You can use choose to use feedback given to you to help you improve your performance, even if it clumsily given.

◆ Teams are likely to experience disagreements and conflicts. Some are likely to be destructive. Ways of dealing with conflict include: avoidance, accommodation, confrontation, compromise, collaboration.

◆ It is important to develop productive relationships with stakeholders – the people who have an interest in your team – by identifying their needs and working out how to meet those needs.

6 Collaboration

Solve problems in the team 96

Clarify the problem 102

Generate options 106

Assess the options 111

Make the decision 116

Implement and review 119

Brian was 100% confident of phoning a friend... knowing that the team was at home with Internet access, a full set of encyclopedias and the Boy's Book of Knowledge

Solve problems in the team

One of the great benefits of effective teams is their ability to combine their resources and collaborate to solve problems and make decisions. This enables the team to learn from its experiences and make improvements in its work.

Any team will encounter a range of problems – difficulties in meeting the requirements of stakeholders, processes that aren't working well, problems in working together as a team to achieve objectives.

Sometimes a problem has an obvious solution that can be implemented straight away. At other times the problem seems difficult to solve. For such a problem, a systematic problem-solving process can be a useful approach.

The stages in a systematic problem-solving process are shown below:

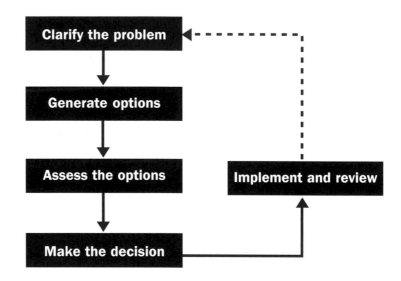

Working through these stages involves a combination of logical, analytical thinking and creative thinking. A range of techniques at each stage can guide your thinking through the process. The next sections of this book take you through each stage.

Although it is perfectly possible to go through these stages and work on the techniques on your own, they can yield better results and be more fun to do in a team:

- Team members can come to a problem from different perspectives, and through the expression and recording of their views and ideas they can:
  - Provide new insights
  - Improve everyone's understanding of the issue
  - Develop fresh approaches to solve the problem
  - Enhance the quality of the decision
  - See how their expertise and experience contributes
  - Learn about each other.

- A contribution from one team member can stimulate a different contribution from another, showing that two or more heads are better than one.

- When team members want to solve a problem they can keep each other going with encouragement, humour and determination to get to the bottom of it.

- By taking joint responsibility to decide how to solve the problem team members are likely to be committed to implementing the decision, and seeing it through.

Joint problem-solving is a product of effective teamworking. But it can also build teamworking, as the team focuses on the real problems it faces and sees the positive effects of collaboration.

To realise these benefits, you must lead the team in:

- Working through the stages and using the various techniques

- Creating an open atmosphere that is based on trust, support and honest open communications

- Expressing their opinions and the reasons for them in a non-defensive way and

- Encouraging everyone to take an active part.

But first, make sure that the problem is one that the team is willing and motivated to sort out.

Can the team solve the problem?

Using any systematic problem-solving process takes time and effort, so it is worth deciding which problems you and your team can most usefully address.

Importance and urgency

Imagine your team is facing a set of problems: at the moment they are vague and you haven't had time to get to grips with them. Without exploring each problem in detail you can describe each one in terms of two key characteristics – importance and urgency:

◆ An important problem is one that has a significant impact on your team's operations or on its abilities to work effectively.

◆ An urgent problem is an issue that is affecting your current work, and is demanding immediate attention.

A simple grid like the one below allows you to show your quick assessment of the importance and urgency of your problems. With this you can identify your priorities and choose how to approach each one.

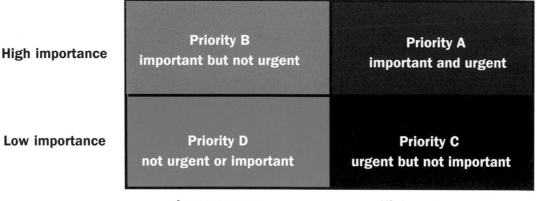

High importance — Priority B: important but not urgent | Priority A: important and urgent

Low importance — Priority D: not urgent or important | Priority C: urgent but not important

Low urgency | High urgency

A A problem in this quadrant is likely to be an emergency or a crisis. It needs dealing with straight away. Because of the pressing need to find a solution to the problem, it may not be realistic to get the team to solve it, as this can take time.

B Problems in this quadrant will have an impact on the team's performance over the long term. If they are not addressed they may become Priority A problems. There is time to engage the team in solving these problems.

C It is important not to allow problems in this quadrant to take up too much time and effort, especially at the expense of those in Priority B. They call for decisive action so you can move on.

D The question for problems in this category is: Do you need to bother with them at all?

A small team in a specialist travel company is responsible for website design and operation. It operates well as a team. The team leader worked with team members to draw up a grid to prioritise their current problems. A slightly edited version of the grid is shown below.

	Low urgency	**High urgency**
High importance	**B** Customer response to new bulletin board Redesign of online brochure Delays in responding to customers' online queries Contract with server provider up for renewal – options?	**A** Blind broken in office so sunlight causing unacceptable glare on screens Customers can't access online booking screens Inadequate cover for helpline support – sickness
Low importance	**D** Dealing with web-hosting company survey	**C** Webcams not operational at Paradise watering hole Report for team meeting next week has not been circulated yet – sickness?

After completing the grid, the team was able to decide how to tackle its Priority A and B problems, and find quick ways of acting on the problems in C. Team members agreed they could start to focus on the first three issues in quadrant B, and report initial progress to the team in two weeks' time. This would enable the team leader to concentrate on sorting out the problems in A, drawing on help from team members as appropriate and keeping them fully informed.

The assessment of relative importance and urgency is subjective and depends on the judgement and interests of those involved. The following questions will help you judge importance and urgency.

Prioritising – importance and urgency

Make a list of the problems your team currently faces – give a short description of the problem so you can identify it. For each problem consider these questions:

◆ What is the impact of the problem on the team?

❖ Is it affecting the team's ability to work together effectively?

❖ Is it affecting the team's ability to achieve its goals?

◆ What will happen if you don't solve the problem:

❖ Now?

❖ In future?

◆ What will happen if you do solve the problem?

Your answers to these questions will help you to place your problems into appropriate quadrants of the grid.

Activity

Use this checklist of questions to categorise the problems facing your team according to importance and urgency, and draw up a grid to identify your priorities.

You could do this on your own or working with team members, depending on their knowledge of problems you face.

You have time to deal with Priority B problems, so you may be able to work with your team to solve them. But check which fall within your team's area of control.

Ownership of the problem

The question of who should take responsibility for the problem is about whether the problem falls within the scope and resources of the team. It also concerns the team's capacity and motivation. This will affect how far you can engage team members to investigate and solve the problem.

Use this checklist of questions to assess how far a problem lies within the scope and reach of the team.

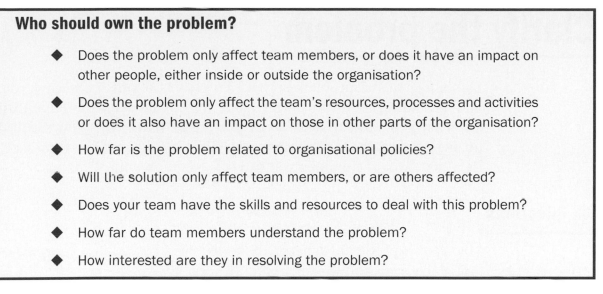

Who should own the problem?

◆ Does the problem only affect team members, or does it have an impact on other people, either inside or outside the organisation?

◆ Does the problem only affect the team's resources, processes and activities or does it also have an impact on those in other parts of the organisation?

◆ How far is the problem related to organisational policies?

◆ Will the solution only affect team members, or are others affected?

◆ Does your team have the skills and resources to deal with this problem?

◆ How far do team members understand the problem?

◆ How interested are they in resolving the problem?

If the effects of a problem stretch beyond the team to other parts of the organisation, it may have to be resolved by others at a different level. In such a case the team should pass the problem to the relevant people, explaining its consequences from the team's perspective.

Problems that sit within the team's responsibility can be resolved within the team. You have to select an appropriate leadership style, depending on the amount of trust and control you can give to the team.

The people who are closest to a problem often know a lot about it and are well-placed to solve it. If they also see the benefits to be gained from solving a problem they are likely to be motivated to investigate and resolve it.

Activity

Use these questions to assess your Priority B problems from the importance/ urgency grid. What are your conclusions? Draw up an action plan that identifies:

◆ Problems that fall within the team's area of responsibility

◆ Problems that can be addressed through team problem-solving

◆ Problems that you should solve and the appropriate leadership style to use in decision-making and communicating

◆ Problems that need to be referred to other parts of the organisation.

Clarify the problem

This stage in the problem-solving process is about increasing your understanding about the problem, identifying its causes and identifying what you want to achieve by solving it. It requires you to think through the issues the problem presents logically and systematically. Here are three techniques you can use to guide your thinking:

Six questions

You can explore all aspects of a problem by asking appropriate questions based on the six main question types:

Why?   **What?**   **How?**   **When?**   **Where?**   **Who?**

The questions below should allow you to plan what information you need to solve a problem. Amend or add to them as appropriate.

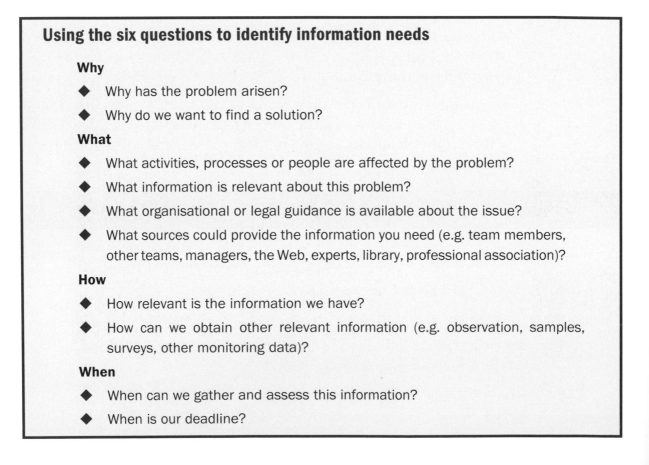

Using the six questions to identify information needs

Why

◆ Why has the problem arisen?

◆ Why do we want to find a solution?

What

◆ What activities, processes or people are affected by the problem?

◆ What information is relevant about this problem?

◆ What organisational or legal guidance is available about the issue?

◆ What sources could provide the information you need (e.g. team members, other teams, managers, the Web, experts, library, professional association)?

How

◆ How relevant is the information we have?

◆ How can we obtain other relevant information (e.g. observation, samples, surveys, other monitoring data)?

When

◆ When can we gather and assess this information?

◆ When is our deadline?

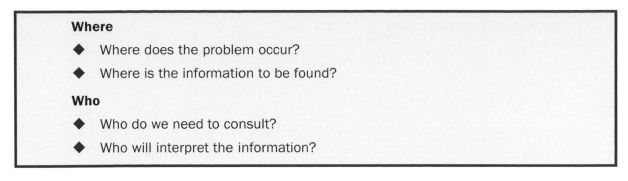

Why-why analysis

The quality of problem-solving depends to a large extent on your team's ability to investigate beyond the obvious causes and develop an appreciation of the underlying ones. Why-why analysis is a simple technique that helps you to dig deeper into the causes. It involves stating a problem and asking 'why', recording the answer, and then asking 'why' of the answer. You go through this process of asking 'why' until you can no longer answer it. The results should uncover the underlying causes and you can begin to analyse them in terms of their importance or significance.

This diagram shows a why-why analysis carried out by the management of a small business to explore the problem of understaffing.

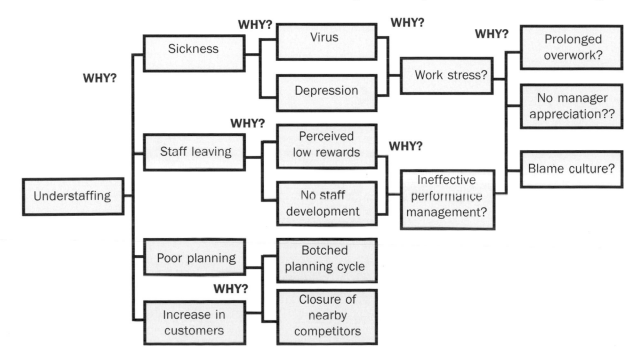

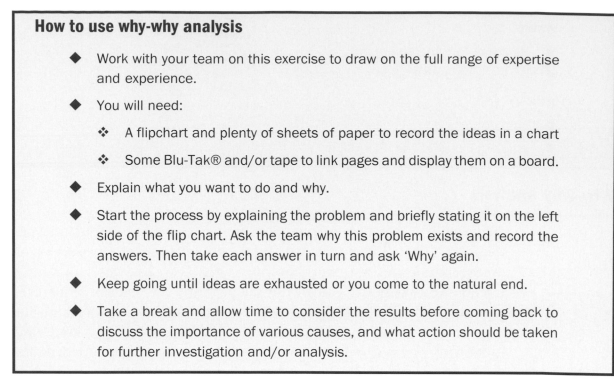

How to use why-why analysis

◆ Work with your team on this exercise to draw on the full range of expertise and experience.

◆ You will need:

❖ A flipchart and plenty of sheets of paper to record the ideas in a chart

❖ Some Blu-Tak® and/or tape to link pages and display them on a board.

◆ Explain what you want to do and why.

◆ Start the process by explaining the problem and briefly stating it on the left side of the flip chart. Ask the team why this problem exists and record the answers. Then take each answer in turn and ask 'Why' again.

◆ Keep going until ideas are exhausted or you come to the natural end.

◆ Take a break and allow time to consider the results before coming back to discuss the importance of various causes, and what action should be taken for further investigation and/or analysis.

Fishbone analysis

This technique is useful for exploring all the dimensions of a problem to find the most significant causes. It is called a fishbone, because the diagram created looks a bit like the skeleton of a fish.

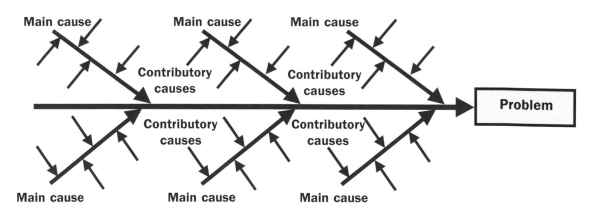

The problem is briefly stated as the head of the fish, and the main causes are noted, forming the ribs off the spine. Then the issues that contribute to these main causes are identified and noted on the small bones connected to the ribs.

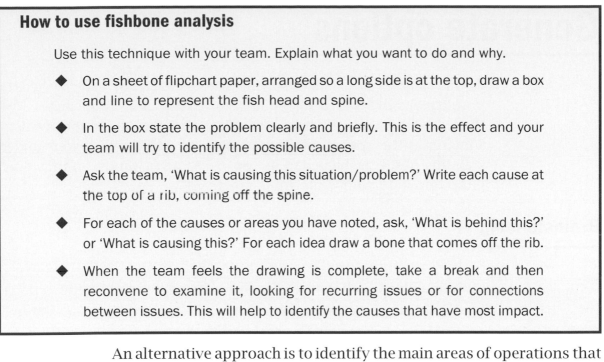

How to use fishbone analysis

Use this technique with your team. Explain what you want to do and why.

◆ On a sheet of flipchart paper, arranged so a long side is at the top, draw a box and line to represent the fish head and spine.

◆ In the box state the problem clearly and briefly. This is the effect and your team will try to identify the possible causes.

◆ Ask the team, 'What is causing this situation/problem?' Write each cause at the top of a rib, coming off the spine.

◆ For each of the causes or areas you have noted, ask, 'What is behind this?' or 'What is causing this?' For each idea draw a bone that comes off the rib.

◆ When the team feels the drawing is complete, take a break and then reconvene to examine it, looking for recurring issues or for connections between issues. This will help to identify the causes that have most impact.

An alternative approach is to identify the main areas of operations that might be contributing to the effect, e.g. people, policies, procedure, materials, methods, machinery. These become the ribs, and you then identify the causes in each area.

Activity

Identify a problem which your team can resolve, and choose one or two of the techniques explored here to use with them.

Plan the session. Allow time to:

◆ Brief the team on the problem and on the technique

◆ Capture and record ideas

◆ Examine the findings

◆ Draw conclusions

◆ Agree what needs to be done next.

Build in some time during the session for a short break. It is also important to allow some time at the end for the team to review how well they worked together, and how useful the technique could be to them in future.

Generate options

By this stage of the problem-solving process the team has analysed the problem and developed a good understanding of its root causes. Now the team has to identify possible options or solutions to the problem. Sometimes the options become obvious as you develop your understanding of the problem and its causes. At other times, options don't jump out and you need to think creatively.

Brainstorming

Brainstorming is a valuable technique that is often used by teams to unleash creativity and generate ideas for solving a problem.

The idea behind brainstorming is to come up with as many ideas as possible in a short space of time. Go for quantity, not quantity: something like 100 ideas in 15 minutes. Ideas can be wild, weird, silly and crazy, as these stimulate other ideas.

> The way that people spark ideas off each other is key to its success.

Every idea is noted and at the end of brainstorming there should be a long list of ideas. Among these ideas there are likely to be some that suggest an interesting or unusual way forward and that may be worth further consideration. Brainstorming should be fun and energising. It involves opening up and being receptive to all ideas. However, most people automatically judge an idea, and this closes down creativity. Creativity and evaluation must be separated to allow creativity to flourish.

To encourage ideas to flow everyone has to follow these rules:

Rules for brainstorming

- Every idea is a good idea, however crazy.
- No criticism is allowed. Do not comment on or ridicule any idea.
- Be spontaneous – speak out when an idea springs to mind.
- Above all, there is no evaluation or judgement. Evaluation comes later.

An essential aspect of creativity is not being afraid to fail.

Dr Edwin Land

Run a brainstorming session

Work with your team. Give any background information the team needs, explain the purpose of the brainstorming session and how it works, and check that they are willing to take part.

- Allow 20 -30 minutes for the session.

- Use a quiet room with a flipchart, flipchart paper, pens and some method for posting flip chart paper on the walls.

- Write the subject for brainstorming at the top of the flip chart. This may be stated as a question, such as 'How can we...?'

- Explain the rules – and post these up on a wall for all to see.

- Appoint a recorder. This person has to be able to write clearly and quickly, recording the ideas word for word, not interpreting them in any way or making any comment. He or she will not have time to contribute his or her own ideas.

- Allow 15 minutes for the session. To warm up you could ask everyone in turn for their first thoughts. When one sheet of flipchart paper is full, post it up on the wall so all the ideas are on view.

- Continue the session until no more ideas are suggested or until the time runs out.

- Take a break so everyone can reflect on the ideas and broaden their thinking. You can then reconvene to order and sort the ideas.

Organising the ideas

The danger of evaluating is to write off the wild or unusual ideas too quickly.

If at first the idea is not absurd, then there is no hope for it.

Albert Einstein

So before evaluating in detail, organise the ideas, making associations and links between them, sorting and grouping them accordingly.

Sort and group the ideas

◆ With your team, decide how to group the ideas. You may see some obvious groupings, e.g. people, equipment, processes. Another approach could be to find broad categories such as easy, difficult, interesting, challenging.

◆ Sort and group the ideas according to your categories, rewriting or rephrasing ideas where appropriate.

◆ When you have grouped ideas you can agree to discard the ones that seem impossible. Be cautious in doing this. First ask, 'How can we make this work?' or use the six questions to check whether an idea has potential.

◆ As a result of sifting, sorting and organising your results you should have a smaller number of ideas to consider and analyse in more detail.

Brainstorming with your team

Brainstorming can be used any time you need to generate ideas with your team. You can use it to practise collaboration skills. If you don't meet face to face you could try brainstorming at a distance:

◆ Use telephone conferencing – someone has to agree to record the ideas and circulate them to everyone afterwards.

◆ Use a chat room on a closed website to run a brainstorm session in real time, or a bulletin board so that people can read team members' ideas and add their own.

◆ Use an Internet phone together with a chat room so that everyone can see a record of the ideas as they are coming.

I've had good results with telephone brainstorming in a small group – there were only four of us. But when you can't see people, it's really important that you trust them...otherwise there's no spontaneity and people hold back.

My experience with using a chat room for brainstorming wasn't so helpful – at one stage ideas were coming thick and fast, with lots of repetition and confusion, and then one person abruptly left the room. That stalled the whole process. We should have set the ground rules a bit more carefully.

Plan and run a brainstorming session with your team to generate ideas for solving a problem. If you have no problem in mind practise brainstorming with your team to develop its collaboration skills. Here are some topics you may want to use:

◆ Ideas for a team logo or motto

◆ Ways to improve team morale and motivation that the team could implement

◆ Ideas for improving customer service – without extra costs.

After the brainstorm session, reflect on what happened.

◆ What role did you play?

◆ How many ideas were generated?

◆ Did everyone obey the rules?

◆ Did everyone contribute equally, or did some people dominate, while others were silent?

◆ How far did team members enjoy the session?

◆ Were the results of the session useful?

◆ What would you do differently next time?

Remember that reflecting on your experience is central to learning from it and doing it better the next time.

Work at creativity

To stimulate creativity you could use:

◆ **Role play** - ask team members to look at the problem from the point of view of fictional or famous people. What ideas would these people bring to the problem?

◆ **Associations** - give team members a random word or picture and ask them to look for links between the problem and the word or picture.

◆ **Metaphor** - ask team members what the problem reminds them of, and then ask them to compare the two issues, looking for similarities and differences.

◆ **Wishful thinking** – ask team members to free themselves from the constraints that surround the problem and imagine ideal solutions. Then look at how you could overcome any obstacles and achieve the ideal solution.

Many people advocate getting away from the normal workplace to stimulate creativity. A different environment can help. Here is what a senior project manager at a telecommunications company said:

I never seem to come up with good ideas in the office. Some of my best ideas have come to me when I've slept on a problem, then wake early and in that half-asleep state my mind is working – I've have some absurd ideas, and some really good ones.

But I've found a couple of other ways that can help. I put the problem at the back of my mind and go for a walk in the country or, for a complete contrast, visit a busy supermarket. The secret seems to be to concentrate on observing what's happening around me. Somehow my mind makes connections with what I'm observing and the problem and a useful idea pops into my head. It doesn't always work of course.

To find out more about creativity you could research 'creative thinking' on the Internet, using a search engine like Google.

Assess the options

At this stage of the problem-solving process you analyse several possible solutions to your problem to find the best one. Don't forget that you always have the option to do nothing.

There are four questions to ask of each option:

◆ **Is it suitable?** Assess the options against agreed goals for success and your constraints.

◆ **Is it feasible?** Do a simple cost-benefit analysis.

◆ **Is it acceptable?** Carry out a stakeholder analysis.

◆ **Can we manage the risks?** Carry out a risk assessment.

Working with your team

Your thinking has to be well-reasoned and consistent, and based on evidence as far as possible. Judgement will be important. By working with your team on the techniques that follow you can draw on a range of experience and perspectives to enhance the quality of the assessment.

Choose an appropriate leadership style in working with your team to assess the options. Consider:

◆ How much knowledge, understanding and experience they have to assess the options

◆ Team members' interest and concern with solving the problem

◆ How much guidance and support you need to give

◆ How much time you have to assess the options with the team.

You may be able to use the techniques in this section to develop the team, to:

◆ Increase collaboration and understanding among members

◆ Increase the team's understanding of the broader context, such as how team goals fit into the organisation, organisational constraints, resources and stakeholder requirements.

Is it suitable?

Consider what you want to achieve in solving the problem and the constraints that limit what you can do or how you can do it. Goals may be related to:

◆ Quality – meeting customer requirements

◆ Efficiency and cost savings

◆ Improving performance and productivity

◆ Improving working relationships

◆ Health and safety

◆ Improving morale and motivation.

Constraints may include legal and organisational policies and regulations and resource availability.

Then simply assess each option by asking whether you think it will meet the goal or the constraint. Judgement comes into play here, but answer 'yes' or 'no' as far as possible.

You can use a chart like the following to record your results:

Will the solution:	Option 1	Option 2	Option 3
Improve quality?			
Produce cost savings?			
Improve working relationships?			
Meet health and safety requirements?			
Conform to quality standards?			

Is it feasible?

To answer this question carry out a simple cost-benefit analysis. This is where you identify all the expected costs and benefits associated with an option, and then assign a value to each. This will help you to find the option which appears to have the greatest benefits and the lowest costs.

How to do a cost-benefit analysis

Take each option in turn. At the top of a sheet of paper, state the option and set up a chart with these four columns:

Quantifiable costs   **Value**   **Quantifiable benefits**   **Value**

List all the costs and benefits that you can quantify or measure in financial terms, e.g. cost of new equipment, cost of training to use new equipment, estimate of benefit of reduced downtime, benefit of reduced running costs. Ignore the 'value' column at this stage.

Then set up another chart with these four columns:

Qualitative costs   **Value**   **Qualitative benefits**   **Value**

In this chart, list the costs and benefits that are difficult to quantify, but which will have an impact on performance. They may include aspects such as motivation, working relationships, levels of satisfaction, skills development.

Now assign values to your costs and benefits. In the first chart work out the financial amount of each cost and benefit listed, and give each one an estimated value. In the second chart assign values from 1–5, where 1 means a low impact on performance and 5 means a high impact on performance. The values here depend largely on judgement, and different team members may well assign different values. You can lead a discussion to reach an agreement. An alternative, quicker approach is to use an average value.

You could lead your team through this analysis, or ask small groups of two or three to complete the analysis and then meet as a team to combine the results and reach agreement. If team members do not have the knowledge and understanding required to assign values, you could lead the team through this part of the analysis, explaining your thinking as you go.

If you can agree the analysis with your team, then it will probably be easier to reach agreement on the decision.

Is it acceptable?

All your team's stakeholders are likely to be affected by the solution – not just your team. So it is important to consider how far different stakeholders will support each option.

Carry out a stakeholder analysis

Identify your stakeholders – customers, suppliers, managers, team members, other groups or teams. For each option, consider these questions:

◆ How does each stakeholder or group benefit?

◆ What are the disadvantages to each group?

◆ How will each stakeholder respond?

◆ What influence or power does each stakeholder or group have?

Review your findings and identify the option that is likely to gain most support from your stakeholders.

The most acceptable option may not necessarily be the one to choose, although it may be the easiest to implement. This analysis will help you to anticipate any difficulties in implementing an option. You may need to plan how to overcome these, perhaps by communicating the benefits, or by seeking active support from influential stakeholders.

Can you manage the risks?

Every decision has risks attached – these are the things that can go wrong. It is important to consider the risks attached to each option. You may find the option with the lowest risks more acceptable. Alternatively you may want to choose a riskier option, because of the greater potential benefits. Either way, by considering the risks you can plan what to do to prevent them from happening, or minimise the impact if they do occur.

Assess the risks

◆ Take each option and draw up a chart with the headings:

Option 1:

Risks	Consequences (1–5)	Likelihood (1–5)	Level of risk

◆ In the first column list the risks by asking 'What can go wrong?'

◆ For each risk consider the possible consequences and rate each from 1–5, where 1 means not significant and 5 means severe.

◆ Now consider the likelihood of the risk occurring. Rate it from 1–5, where 1 is not likely and 5 is very likely.

◆ Work out the level of each risk by multiplying its consequences by its likelihood.

◆ Highlight those risks with the highest scores. These are what you perceive to be the greatest risks.

◆ Consider what you can do to avoid or minimise these risks to lower the level of risk.

◆ Compare the total level of risk for each option to identify the option with the lowest level of risk.

Activity

Plan to work with your team to assess the options for solving a problem, using:

◆ Assessment against goals and constraints

◆ Cost-benefit analysis

◆ Stakeholder analysis

◆ Risk assessment.

Review the experience:

◆ The usefulness of each of these techniques

◆ The effectiveness of teamworking in using these techniques

◆ Your contribution and leadership.

Identify what went well and what you want to improve next time.

After assessing options with these techniques, you may have a clear winner on which everyone can agree. Then the decision is straightforward. However, the assessment may not deliver an obvious solution. In such a case decision-making may require more effort. We look at decision-making in teams in the next section.

Make the decision

There are three main approaches to decision-making in teams:

◆ Team leader takes the final decision

◆ Consensus

◆ Voting.

Team leader makes the decision

This is often the fastest way of making a decision, but consider the following:

◆ If team members have engaged in joint problem-solving will they be demoralised if you take the final decision?

◆ How do team members expect the decision to be made?

◆ How much responsibility are team members prepared to take for making the decision?

◆ How far will team members support a decision made by you?

Consensus

Reaching a consensus is where team members make a shared, agreed decision. Consensus means that all team members give their full backing and support to a decision and its implementation. For this reason it is very valuable in teamworking.

Building a consensus takes time. It may emerge from the process of joint problem-solving. But when there are different views on the best solution, you could invite team members to take part in consensus building, where they work together to explore and discuss the issues with the aim of agreeing a joint decision.

To do this effectively team members must agree to draw on key teamworking skills:

◆ Listening attentively

◆ Explaining their own position and their reasoning

- Behaving in a non-defensive way

- Being prepared to challenge constructively and respond constructively

- Checking that everyone shares the same understanding of language used – for example, what do people mean by 'short term' – is it a week or a year?

- Being open-minded

- Being cooperative.

As a team leader you can act as a facilitator: supporting open, two-way communications, linking ideas, seeking clarification, summarising progress, encouraging contributions, reminding people of objectives.

Voting

Voting takes less time than consensus building, and it can be carried out in a democratic way. Voting may provide a way out of an impasse, when the team can't reach agreement. But a decision that is based on a vote may not carry the full support of the team.

Put options to a vote

- Explain why you are asking the team to vote and check that they support the principle of voting.

- Summarise the problem and what has been done so far to solve it.

- Describe the remaining options for solving it and give each option a short name for easy identification.

- Give team members a sheet of paper and ask them to work on their own to identify their preferred options by giving each a score: 1 is the most preferred option, 2 is the second best, 3 is the next best, and so on.

- Ask team members to submit their 'voting paper'.

- Add up the scores for each option to find the one that has most support – the one with the lowest score.

Difficulties with team decision-making

Working in a team can create two interesting conditions that can get in the way of effective decision-making.

◆ **Groupthink**. This is where being part of the team and conforming to its norms and consensus become more important than individual judgement. The team may make poor decisions because it assumes it is right.

◆ **Risky shift**. This is where the team takes greater risks than its members would ordinarily take. This may be because the team members share responsibility for the decision, so no one feels personally responsible.

The dangers of groupthink

I experienced groupthink in a sales team I belonged to when I worked for a newspaper group. When we went into a meeting we used to park our critical faculties outside!

The team was close-knit and we had an excellent team spirit, possibly because we had achieved extremely good sales figures. But I think that made us feel invulnerable and dismissive of people outside the team.

The team came apart when we ran a competition designed to boost sales. It did this very successfully – not surprising, really, given that the competition was too easy to win, and the prize was an expensive holiday in the Caribbean. The team was responsible: the competition was poorly designed; it didn't even meet basic legal guidelines. The company was left wide open, it lost a lot of money, and had to go into damage limitation mode.

Being aware of the dangers of groupthink and the risky shift phenomenon can go some way in protecting a team from them. These potential problems highlight the need to welcome constructive disagreement and to encourage the expression of divergent opinions.

Implement and review

A decision can't be judged a good decision until it is put into action, and is seen to work.

Implementation and review is the last part of the process of problem-solving. It involves carrying out the decision, and then reviewing its effectiveness in a formal review. If this highlights difficulties or opportunities, you may decide to start the process afresh.

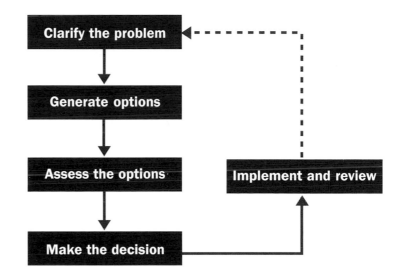

Reviewing the consequences of a decision is important. It lets the team stand back from the process of problem-solving and implementation to examine how the decision was put into action, the successes and shortcomings in the results and the lessons to be learned.

Activity

Plan to review the implementation of a decision with your team. You could:

◆ Use the tips on reviewing given in 'Focus on the task' in Chapter 3 on Team performance.

◆ Draw on ideas for running a team meeting in Chapter 4 on Communications. For example, you may find the six hats thinking technique useful for managing the discussion.

- ◆ Where appropriate, use techniques for problem-solving given in this section

- ◆ Ask for feedback from your team on your performance in running the session.

Summarise the results of the review session. In particular, consider what lessons your team has learned which you can apply:

- ◆ When you next make a decision

- ◆ When you next carry out a review.

Reviews enable the team to learn and improve. This is crucial for effective teamwork.

Summary

- ◆ Think about how and when you can encourage team members to collaborate in problem-solving and decision-making.

- ◆ Use a range of techniques to help team members collaborate effectively to:

  - ❖ Clarify the problem – six questions, why-why analysis, fishbone analysis

  - ❖ Generate options – brainstorming, think creatively

  - ❖ Assess the options – cost-benefit analysis, stakeholder analysis, risk assessment

  - ❖ Make the decision – team leader decides, reaching consensus, voting. But beware of the risky shift phenomenon and groupthink.

  - ❖ Review the effectiveness of the decision that is implemented and the problem-solving process itself.

Index

A

Agenda 61
Arguments 68

B

Belbin's team roles 24
Brainstorming 106
Building effective teams 4

C

Celebrate success 47
Chairing skills 64
Chairperson 62
Coaching 45
Collaboration 96
Communications
    open 52, 77
    planning tool 51
    and technology 69
    process 50
Compromise 87
Conflict 86
Consensus 116
Constructive feedback 82
Contract 27
Control 80
Controlling 41
Cost-benefit analysis 112
Creative thinking 106
Creativity 109
Customers 31, 90

D

Decision-making 116
Development 45
Diversity 7
    in team membership 13
    value in 13

E

Email 69

F

Facilitator 62
Feedback 82
Fishbone analysis 104

G

Goals 31
Groupthink 86, 118

H

Hidden agendas 66
Hierarchy of objectives 33

I

Importance and urgency grid 98
Induction 46

J

Johari window 77

L

Leadership 15
    functions 17
    role model 80
    style 38, 80, 111
Learning 45
Listening 53

M

Management 15
Meeting rules 60
Mentoring 45
Mission 32
Monitoring 41
Motivation 35

O

Objectives 39
    hierarchy 33
Open communications 52

P

Participation 37
Planning 41
Problem-solving 87
    assess the options 111
    clarifying 102
    generate options 106
    implement and review 119
    make the decision 116
    systematic 96
Problems
    ownership 100
    prioritising 98
Project teams 9
Purpose 31

Q

Quality improvement teams 11
Questioning skills 57

R

Relationships 53, 77
Resources 44
Responsibility 37
Review 119
Reviewing 41
Risk assessment 114
Risky shift 118
Running the meeting 61

S

Self-managed teams 11
Situational leadership model 38
Six questions technique 102

SMART objectives 39
Stages of development 20
Stakeholder analysis 90, 113
Stakeholders 89
Strategy 32
Success, celebrating 47
Suppliers 31, 90
Support 43

T

Team contract 27
Team meetings 59
    barriers to effectiveness 59
    difficult situations 66
Team performance 30
Team purpose 31
Team roles 23
Teams 2
    benefits 3
    drawbacks 3
Technology 69
Teleconferencing 71
Trust 77
Trustworthy behaviour 81
Type of team 7

V

Value 32
Videoconferencing 73
Virtual teams 12
Vision 32
Voting 117

W

Web-based discussion 74
Why-why analysis 103
Work groups 7
Work teams 7